DON'T BE INTIMIDATED!

HOW TO CONFIDENTLY SELL TO EXECUTIVES

HEALTH CARE EDITION

Tom Komer and Buster Brown

Printed in the United States of America

07 06 05 04   010   1 2 3 4 5

Cover Photo and Author Photos by Shannon Drawe
Illustrations by Leslie Kregel
Book Design by Crystal Wood

ISBN 0-9752543-1-6

Published by
EXECON LTD
122 Hughes Lane
Mooresville, NC 28117
704-664-7900
execon@msn.com

WHO SHOULD READ THIS BOOK

If you have gotten this far, that means that you have a curiosity about what this book can do for you or your company. It also means that you believe there is some room to improve or add to those abilities.

The bottom line for this book is that it is written to really make a difference in the selling abilities of sales representatives who sell capital goods and services. It's a no-nonsense approach with very practical techniques for getting to and impressing executives. It will not take a lot of effort for you to read.

But, it could take a lot of effort to change your behavior to internalize the techniques and to customize them to your style and territory. There are plenty of examples and tips in the book to help in this process.

The book is based on many years of selling and consulting by the authors, much of it done at executive levels. We know that what is presented here works because we have lived most of our adult lives practicing it.

It does not matter how experienced or inexperienced you might be. You could be new to selling or have 20 years under your belt. This book works for everyone.

We readily agree that there are some good folks out there who can add plenty of their own executive selling techniques to what is contained in here. We encourage them to use the book to mentor those who are not so skilled, adding their own experiences to the book's techniques.

It does not matter if you sell to for-profit hospitals, not-for-profits, or governmental hospitals. Again, the book works if you are *selling capital goods and services.*

Not convinced? Then, look at the table of contents and check out the "Key Points" at the end of some of the chapters. That will give you a solid taste of what is here for you.

To make the book easy to read, we have used a literary device. This is not a dry dissertation. We wanted it to be a fast read and a fun read for busy sales reps.

When you start reading, you will be introduced to Joe Repp, our quintessential salesman who has lots to learn. His mentor is a ghost, Sely Sharpe...yes, we know it's corny, but it's also fun and a lot less boring than many sales skill books. Through their interaction and experiences, you are immersed into the learning along with Joe. And, like Joe, we trust you will develop your own knowledge, skills and attitude to be a winner at the top of your prospect accounts.

Being a winner at this top rung can create big differentiation between you and your competitors. It's an opportunity to differentiate not only by *what* you sell, but also *how* you sell.

It also helps you to truly fulfill the promise of selling: meeting the needs of people and hospitals...at the executive level.

Have fun, and good selling!

ABOUT THE AUTHORS

TOM KOMER

Since 1972, Tom Komer has been a consultant specializing in strategic planning, sales and marketing, and sales and sales management training, primarily for high-tech industries with particular focus on information systems providers. For the first eight of those years, he was Vice President of Development for Tratec, Inc., a publicly-held consulting and training company in Los Angeles, CA, and President of Tratec International, headquartered in London, UK. When McGraw-Hill acquired Tratec in 1979, Tom started his own consultancy, EXECON LTD, which continues to the present.

Tom works with a variety of companies around the world ranging from the Fortune 100 to small, independent resellers. He serves as a director on the boards of public and private companies.

Tom has been instrumental in the success of both private and public companies through his thought leadership and his pragmatic approach to business. Thousands of sales representatives have experienced his highly intensive training programs. He is known for helping his clients with very practical and useful advice by telling them what they need to hear, not what they want to hear.

Prior to his consultancy activities, he was in sales and field management for Scientific Data Systems which became part of Xerox Corporation in 1969. He was a programmer and applied mathematician in the aerospace industry prior to these experiences.

Tom has established himself as the "go-to person" for many companies and executives around the globe for no nonsense, practical sales and marketing advice.

BUSTER BROWN

Buster Brown is a very successful salesman and sales leader in the technology industry. Over his career, he has directly sold millions of dollars worth of computer software and services and has managed sales organizations that have accounted for over $2 billion in sales. He was instrumental in building one of the top 10 global software companies in record time. He now devotes all of his expertise, thought leadership and entrepreneurial talent to his sales consultancy and recruiting firm, which is focused specifically on software sales talent.

Buster is known for taking tough situations and turning them around. For example, at Platinum Technology, he took the company's worst performing region and implemented a complete turnaround including upgrading nearly all the sales reps and implementing a rigid funnel management program. These changes resulted in that region becoming a high-performer within 18 months. He was also responsible for creating and implementing a very successful global accounts program that ultimately accounted for over 10% of Platinum's annual revenue.

Having integrated sales organizations of more than 70 acquisitions in five years while at Platinum, Buster and his sales management team helped make Platinum one of the most recognized entrepreneurial success stories, growing from a startup to the eighth largest software enterprise in the world and quickly reaching $1 billion in revenue. Platinum was acquired in 1999 by Computer Associates.

In 1999, Buster was one of the founders of divine interVentures, inc., an Internet business-to-business incubator and venture capital company. In 2000, he founded SaleSpring, a global business providing sales consultation, sales out-tasking and reseller services to Internet startups. SaleSpring was acquired by divine, inc., in 2001. Buster was named Executive Vice President at divine, inc., where he was responsible for over $500 million in software and services sales.

Before Platinum Technology and divine, Buster served in various sales management and sales positions with Computer Associates, Boole & Babbage, Software Recording Corp., and Confirm Ventures, a venture capital organization.

His experience and sales savvy have earned him a reputation as a premier sales strategist.

HOW THIS BOOK IS ORGANIZED

CHAPTERS: Each chapter introduces a set of knowledge and skills useful in calling on executives. The chapters build on each other and reinforce previous content.

REVIEW KEY POINTS: At the end of each chapter, there is a short list of the key points made in the chapter. This list can serve as a reminder for those who have read the book and want to go back to reinforce their knowledge and skills.

DISCUSSION TOPICS: To transfer the knowledge and techniques to the real world, each chapter has a series of questions to consider. These questions can be considered by an individual, or they can form the basis of discussions at sales meetings in the local office or at training sessions.

EXECUTIVE QUOTES: Scattered throughout the book are quotes from real executives. These quotes put the points made in the chapters squarely into the real world. We identify the executive's position, but not his or her name.

You will find some of the executives don't agree in their comments. That just emphasizes the need for you to be flexible and creative in how you sell to executives. If a technique or strategy doesn't work for a particular person, it might work for another.

Here is one of many executive quotes to whet your appetite for what you will read:

I loved your book and wish that every representative that I dealt with would read it and follow the suggestions that you have made.

Vice President, Marketing
Airline

TABLE OF CONTENTS

WHO SHOULD READ THIS BOOK iii

ABOUT THE AUTHORS v

HOW THIS BOOK IS ORGANIZED ix

CHAPTER 1:
YET ANOTHER BOOK
ON SELLING TO EXECUTIVES 1
    The Lament of Joe Repp
    Sound Familiar?
    Meet Joe's Coach
    Test Yourself
    Review Key Points
    Discussion Topics

CHAPTER 2:
WHAT EXECUTIVES DO FOR A LIVING 19
    Empathy: the Most Critical Tool
    One-half of an Executive's Job: Worrying
    The Other Half of an Executive's Job:
        Making Decisions
    Review Key Points
    Discussion Topics

CHAPTER 3:
DO YOUR HOMEWORK 43
    Why Do the Work?
    You Are an Expert
    What to Look for
    A Goldmine of Information: The Annual
        Report's Letter to the Shareholders

How to Use this Strategic Information
More Business Intelligence
Review Key Points
Discussion Topics

CHAPTER 4:
WHO TO SEE AND WHEN **81**
Do You Really Need to Call at the "C" Level?
Who to Visit
Timing Is Important
Review Key Points
Discussion Topics

CHAPTER 5:
GETTING THE APPOINTMENT **107**
Why Is it So Hard to Get an Executive
  Appointment?
The "Who" and the "What" of Getting an
  Executive Appointment
A Compelling Introductory Letter
Review Key Points
Discussion Topics

CHAPTER 6:
PREPARING FOR A DYNAMITE
EXECUTIVE MEETING **127**
>Your Research Is the Font of Ideas
>References: Your Proof Statement
>A Compelling Opening
>Good Questions to Ask
>How Long to Meet
>Know the Person
>Be Prepared in Many Ways
>Review Key Points
>Discussion Topics

CHAPTER 7:
HOW TO CONDUCT
THE EXECUTIVE CALL **155**
>Have an Attitude
>What to Expect
>"Execu-speak 101"
>Review Key Points

CHAPTER 1:
YET ANOTHER BOOK ON SELLING TO EXECUTIVES

THE LAMENT OF JOE REPP

"**I**'m getting killed! My biggest opportunity ever. Going down the drain. Killed by the bad guys at Super Solutions. I just know we're better for Churchill's needs. So our price may be a little higher than Super Solutions. It's all about real return on investment, right? They've just got to see that, don't they? Why have they shut me out?"

So muses Joe Repp, sales representative for Mega Systems. Joe is relatively new to selling...about nine months now. He came over to sales from the technical side. His manager thought he would be a sure success, given all his technical knowledge about Mega's products and customers' needs. He did quite well in all his sales training classes. And, to be sure, Joe has an outgoing personality that's hard to resist.

But, here he is, losing his first big opportunity to the competition. Joe is virtually locked out from speaking to any of his contacts at Churchill Hospital. They tell him that, now that the proposals have been submitted, hospital rules exclude any vendor contacts until the decision is made.

Joe has been able to keep in contact with one of the technical evaluators on the selection committee. He and Sam were very simpatico with a deep love of talking technical. Sam has been keeping Joe abreast of the situation at Churchill. While no one else is taking Joe's calls, apparently the rep from Super Solutions isn't having any problem meeting with key members of the committee and with the brass at Churchill. According to Sam, Joe's proposal looks like it's headed to the round file.

"I did what I was supposed to do. I called high and broad, meeting with every committee member. I spent lots of time with the technical evaluators educating them on how to apply the MegaDoppel to their business. My meeting with Bob, the committee head, although short, was certainly friendly. I asked him how I was doing compared to the other supplier his team was looking at. He encouraged me to continue working with the technical people. That's something of an endorsement, right?

Now, what do you think that guy from Super Solutions is doing with the brass at Churchill? I wouldn't know what to say to them, even if I could get an appointment."

SOUND FAMILIAR?

Poor Joe. Excellent product...knows his product inside and out...knows how his product impacts the prospect's operations...nice guy...but, still, he is outmaneuvered by the competition at the executive level of his prospect.

We can all empathize with Joe. At some point in our careers, we have all been there. Some of you reading this book may feel you are still there to some degree. That's why you are spending your valuable time to read this book in the hope of picking up a useful point or two that will give you that special edge.

Well, we'll do our best not to disappoint you. This isn't a generic book of "feel-good" ideas, full of banalities and platitudes about how to be a successful salesperson. This book is real world. Why? Because, when you make sales calls at the executive levels of your prospects, they don't have the time or patience for those banalities and platitudes. They are primarily interested in how you are going to make them and their businesses successful. You can leave the cute stuff in the lobby.

What you will read here are the true thoughts and feelings of executives about salespeople. We will share techniques and strategies which really work to deal with and leverage those executive views. You will also read how to personalize these tips and techniques to your own selling style and selling environment.

Big promise? Yes. And you will quickly see if we can deliver on that promise.

To do so, we're going to use a literary construct...a ghost...who is going to coach Joe in the skills, knowledge and attitude that can make him successful calling on the executive suites and, thereby, considerably enhancing his competitive position. A ghost, you say? Yep, corny, but effective. And, it makes the reading more interesting than a dry exposition.

Let's get back to Joe and we'll show you what we mean. You'll recognize Joe's special coach in the interchanges. He is the one who speaks in *italics*. Interesting skill, hmm?

As Joe continues to wallow in his self-pity, he has a sudden visitor...

MEET JOE'S COACH

"Maybe I should have stayed in technical support. I was good. Everyone respected me. Now, as a sales rep, I feel like a failure. I just can't seem to do what it takes to win the big deals. I'm petrified at calling on an executive and looking stupid. What am I going to say? Look how fast our MegaDoppel goes? Or, let me show you some neat tricks you can do with the MegaDoppel? That stuff interests techies, but executives?

I wish there was some sort of magician who could wave a magic wand and give me what it takes to succeed with the heavy-hitters."

"You called?"

"Who said that?"

"I did."

"Where are you?"

*"Right here,
in front of you!"*

"What? Who are you? How did you get in here?"

"Well, it would have been easier if the door wasn't locked. As to who I am, I'm who you just asked for, although I don't consider myself a magician. I'm just someone who has lots of good selling experiences. I try to inspire others to be great sales reps who consistently close orders. I try to make them over-quota achievers."

"I don't believe you. Get out of here! Can't you see I'm busy.?"

"OK, if you don't want my help to do it right, then you can continue to stumble and fumble your way through selling. Many like you have likewise turned a deaf ear to me. I'll just go find someone else who is willing to listen. Maybe that guy selling for Super Solutions who is beating the pants off you at Churchill might be an interesting subject. See you around, Joe, although I don't see how you'll be around much longer."

"Wait a second. What do you know about Churchill and that jerk selling for Super Solutions?"

"Well, I know that, given your current strategy and position in the deal, you don't have a ghost of a chance to win. Excuse the pun.

I also know that you lost this deal long ago and didn't even know it. The Super Solution sales rep had it sewn up early in the opportunity when he met with Churchill's Vice President of Operations and showed her how Super Solutions' system was tailored to enhance several of her key initiatives to increase productivity at Churchill. So, as they say in the movies, 'Hasta la vista, chump.' "

"How did you learn about that productivity stuff with the VP? I never heard about that?"

"Of course, you didn't. You were too busy with the techies showing off how smart you were with your MegaDoppel. In the meantime, bigger things were happening up top at Churchill...a place where you've never been, but where the Super Solutions guy was."

"But the technical evaluation committee makes the decision on what Churchill should buy. I was focusing my efforts on them."

"Yes, you're right. Selection committees often chose what solutions a hospital will buy, as long as that selection fits into the broader mandate given to the committee by the senior executives. Just as often, the committee might recommend a particular solution as being the best or preferred, but the hospital buys something else because there are bigger things at stake. In those cases, the job of the committee is to identify which solutions pass the technical qualifications, but the senior executives can override the committee's preferred solution as long as the one the hospital buys passes technical muster.

It's not uncommon for the decision to have already been made even before a committee is formed. The selection committee is then just an exercise to follow the hospital's procurement process. How do you know that this isn't the case at Churchill? Maybe that 'jerk' at Super Solutions isn't so much of a jerk, after all?"

"I don't believe that. They've spent too much time with me if they had already decided on Super Solutions before they even started. And, I still think that guy at Super Solutions is a jerk."

"Maybe you're right, Joe. For the moment, let's assume you are...about the committee being a legitimate investigation.

Sometimes the overriding reason to buy something less than the technically greatest is price, or delivery, or support considerations. Maybe more often, it's a strong personal preference born out of an executive having more trust and confidence in one supplier versus the others. Minimizing the risks of doing business is a major responsibility of executives.

People buy from people. People usually buy from those they trust and have confidence in...people who will fulfill their end of the deal. This factor is possibly the most important decision criterion. It can easily surpass technical and price considerations.

But, I guess you know better, so you don't need me. 'Bye."

"Wait! Wait! How do you know all this stuff?"

"Let's just say that I float around, observing what goes on in executive offices."

"But how can you help me? I'm sure my boss will fire me as soon as he learns that the Churchill deal is down the drain. He was counting on that deal to make his quarterly numbers. He made Churchill a high profile piece of business to win. Now, we'll all look stupid to our own big brass, and I'm sure I'll be the first sacrificial lamb to get the axe."

"Well, maybe we can do something about that. Maybe we can reverse the Churchill situation and turn you into a winner instead of a whiner. A famous baseball manager once coined an observation that certainly applies here — 'It ain't over until it's over!'

But you're going to have to carefully listen to me and have the courage to try some new things. Some of those things will involve the personal risk of looking dumb or of failing. Are you willing to make that effort and take those risks?"

"I can't look any dumber than I do now. And, I'm already pretty sure that my career as a sales rep is coming to an end. If you can help me, I'll do as you say."

"No, I don't want you to be a robot doing what I say. I want you to be a thinking business representative who understands why and how hospitals make decisions to invest in products and services. But, more than that, I want you to understand how executives and their subordinates make those decisions.

As I said earlier, people buy from people. It's how effective you are at the 'belly to belly' skills with the right people at your prospect that has the most impact on your success. This all assumes that you have a solution which satisfies the prospect's minimum buying criteria. And, your price can't be so beyond the prospect's budget or your competitor's price that they just can't justify buying from you no matter how good a sales rep you are.

I'll also assume you already know how to sell to technical evaluators, although we'll probably have to spend some time refining your techniques there, as well. What we'll focus on is when and how to call on the executives at a prospect account...what turns them on and what turns them off...how to win their respect and support.

Now, this is no guarantee that you'll win every time. It does give you a better chance of influencing the decision and differentiating yourself from the competition.

Don't think that you have to call on executives in every opportunity. Some deals are clearly a technical or a price decision. Either you have the best widget or you don't get the business. Or, you have the lowest price or you lose.

Part of your challenge as an effective business representative is to know what are the real decision criteria in a deal.

It's generally a safe strategy to call at the top in every deal, assuming you have the skills to do so and don't alienate any of the subordinates by 'going around them to the boss.' There's a skill in keeping those lower folks positive about you calling high.

So, you see, we have a lot to talk about, and you have a lot to learn and try. Are you ready to do it?"

"I guess so. As I said, what do I have to lose. If you can help me to turn around Churchill, I'll be a hero!"

"We'll see about Churchill.

First, there's something you must clearly understand. Aside from ethical issues, there are no right and wrong ways to sell. The only black and white I know about in selling is, 'Did you get the order?' Some of my previous students have said, 'Did we get paid for the order?' Others added, 'Did I get the commission check?'

The real issue with what you are going to learn is what are the risks and benefits of using a particular technique or strategy? How can you minimize the risks and maximize the benefits? How can you tailor that technique or strategy to your personal style?

I'm not trying to change who you are. I'm trying to change what you do: give you new knowledge and new skills to expand your selling toolkit. With those new tools, you'll change your own attitude.

Is this understood?"

"Yeah, I guess so. Let's just see where all this takes us.

What do I call you, anyway? And, what makes you think you're so smart?"

"Well, Joe, as I said, I float around a lot and see lots of sales reps, some good, some not so good. I used to be a sales rep, myself. I started in grammar school, selling newspaper and magazine subscriptions. I worked my way through college by selling.

When I graduated, I immediately took a selling job with one of the big office equipment manufacturers. What a great learning experience, going from door to door in big buildings!

After several years of doing that...by the way, I blew out my quota each year...I joined a company which sold capital goods and services. That's where my sales career really bloomed. I worked with many hospitals across all levels of those hospitals, helping them to solve important problems...helping them to turn around bad situations...helping them to be more successful with patient care and in operating efficiently.

That's what selling is about, Joe. Helping others. It's like you're a doctor examining patients and prescribing treatments. I loved it. Made the 100% Club every year, usually in the top five.

It all ended one day, when I was fumbling in my car for a pen while talking on a cell phone. I rounded a curve too tightly and met an 18-wheeler. Fortunately, the truck driver wasn't hurt. My car was squished like an accordion. I never knew what happened. But, at least, I had the satisfaction of knowing I had closed that big order at Mercy Hospital. I was trying to copy down the purchase order number when I had the accident.

Now, the Big Boss up there lets me come down occasionally to visit with other reps like you. He figures that, since I have all these techniques and experience, I could continue to do some good helping others. So, here I am to help you.

By the way, my name was Selwin Sharpe. You can just call me Sely."

"Sely. I might have known."

"OK, Joe Repp, now if you're ready, let's get to the first lesson of executive selling: understanding what executives do for a living."

TEST YOURSELF

Here is a little self-test to help you determine where you are in terms of being effective in selling to executives. Below each question is the general skill that the question tests. All of these skills are developed throughout this book. Be honest in your answers. Only you will see the results.

Rate yourself for each question using a scale of 1-5, where...

5 = No problem at all; happens all the time

4 = Do a good job most of the time; rarely slip; happens most of the time

3 = Not bad, but not great; do a reasonable job; happens occasionally

2 = Definitely can improve; doesn't happen often

1 = Do a horrible job; rarely happens, if ever; need lots of help

---

_____ 1. Are you able to get appointments with executives with whom you have never met?

Skill: Ability to get appointments with executives

_____ 2. Do you think you meet with executives often enough for what you sell and where you sell?

Skill: How and when to use executives in a sales campaign

_____ 3. Are you able to get follow-up appointments with executives with whom you have met only once?

Skill: Being impressive enough in the first call to be able to get a second visit

_____ 4. When you meet with an executive, are you comfortable talking with the executive about his or her job challenges?

Skill: Being able to use "execu-speak" and understanding the executive's drivers, strategies and critical success factors

_____ 5. When an executive talks about his/her business, do you understand what the executive is talking about?

Skill: Understanding the executive's business from his/her perspective and how you can impact that business

_____ 6. Do executives open up in discussions with you, sharing confidential information?

Skill: Ability to gain the trust and confidence of an executive

_____ 7. When you meet with executives, do they do most of the talking?

Skill: Ability to ask good questions and to listen

_____ 8. Can you readily express what benefits your product/services will provide in terms of the executive's job responsibilities?

> *Skill:* Ability to present your products/ services in terms of the executive's drivers, strategies and critical success factors

_____ 9. Will an executive readily accept your telephone call to discuss an issue you have raised?

> *Skill:* Ability to gain the interest of an executive with a compelling opening statement and then to develop trust and confidence on the part of the executive in your value to him/her

_____ 10. Do executives call you to solicit your input on issues?

> *Skill:* Ability to develop trust and confidence in your value as a knowledgeable business consultant

_____ 11. Do you consider yourself a source of information to executives?

> *Skill:* Ability to understand business from an executive's perspective and staying current in your business research

_____ 12. Do you pay enough attention to building relationships with the administrative assistants of executives?

> *Skill:* Ability to work with the executive's right-hand person

You should have scored **4** or **5** for each question. Any score less than 4 should be a particular area of focus for you as you progress through this book.

REVIEW KEY POINTS

1. Aside from ethics, there are no black and whites in selling. The thing to consider in using a particular selling technique or strategy is how to maximize the benefits and minimize the risks in that situation.

2. People buy from people. How you establish trust and confidence in you, your company and your products and services with each important person in the opportunity does more to define who will win than any other factor...assuming your product and services pass the minimum buying criteria and are not totally out of the realm of the prospect's budget or too high compared to the competition's price.

3. Selling capital products and services is usually multi-layered and multi-dimensional. It's a thinking person's business to effectively sell high and broad.

4. Not all opportunities require calling on a prospect's higher management. But, in general, it's a useful strategy to create a bias for you and your solutions.

DISCUSSION TOPICS

1. How important is calling on executives in your selling? Do you need to call on them often? Why or why not?

2. How do you feel about calling on executives? What do you find easy? Hard? What techniques have you found that consistently work, either to get an appointment with an executive, or to win an executive's support for you and what you are selling?

3. What happened in the last sales call you made to an executive whom you had never met before? What did you learn from that experience relative to selling techniques at the executive level?

I am shocked, but I don't get that many salespeople calling on me. I get tons of marketing material, but very little direct communication from salespeople. I think they are scared to call me.

President
Aluminum Window Manufacturer

CHAPTER 2:
WHAT EXECUTIVES
DO FOR A LIVING

EMPATHY: THE MOST CRITICAL TOOL

"*OK, Joe, our journey to selling success in the executive office begins with a simple concept, but not so simple to do. It's called empathy. Do you know what empathy is, Joe?*"

"Sure. It's putting yourself into the other guy's shoes to see the world as he sees it."

The most successful sales folks selling to me know my business well, but just as importantly they know my industry. They also know what it is like to walk in my shoes.

Vice President, Operations
Financial Investment
Company

"*Right. To sell to executives, you have to have empathy with them.*"

"C'mon, Sely, that's a ridiculous expectation. I know about trying to relate to my prospect, but how am I going to have empathy with an executive...any executive, including that VP of Operations at Churchill. If I was able to have empathy with them, I would be one of them!"

"*No, Joe. As you very astutely observed, empathy is putting yourself in the other person's shoes. It doesn't mean those shoes have to fit, or that you are able to walk in them. What it does mean is that you can see their point of view. That's what you are now going to learn to do."*

"This I've got to see. All right, Mr. Smart Guy, teach me empathy with executives."

ONE HALF OF AN EXECUTIVE'S JOB: WORRYING

"Pay close attention. I'll be very explicit. Ask questions if you don't understand any point.

In the great scheme of business, executives get paid to do two things: worry and make decisions based on those worries.

We'll start with the worries. Now, as I go through these worries, you should be thinking about how you, your company or your products and services can directly impact an executive's worries. It's got to be direct, because if you can help an executive to cope with a significant worry, then that executive will be interested in talking with you.

To help you to understand this concept, I have divided the executive worries into six categories. And, we'll use that VP of Operations at Churchill and some other executives as examples to put this concept into real life."

"I think I'm already ahead of you. My VP of Sales is worried about me closing the Churchill deal. I can certainly have an impact on that one! And, if the second part is taking action on that worry, I already know what that's going to be."

"Yes, Joe, that's actually a good example. The Churchill order is strategically important to your own VP of Sales. We'll be dealing with that shortly. But first, let's broaden the idea of executive worries.

The first category is financial worries. What do you think is the number one concern of any executive regardless of title when it comes to financial worries?"

"Well, if it's a for-profit hospital like Churchill, I guess the number one worry is making a profit."

"Profit is certainly in this category. But, there is a bigger worry that has more significant impact on an enterprise, especially in the short-term. It's called cash flow.

In our free-enterprise system, if you don't have cash or its equivalent, called credit, you simply can't play in the game of business. For a hospital, cash flow is called just that: cash flow. For a department or operation within a hospital, whether it be for-profit, not-for-profit or governmental, it's called budget.

No cash, no budget, no play. Do you understand that, Joe?"

"Yeah, sure. It applies beyond hospitals. If I don't have cash or credit, I'll have a hard time making ends meet or doing the things I want to do. This is definitely a situation I've been thinking about, big time, lately."

"Yes, many of these concepts have parallels in our daily lives which makes them easier to understand and easier to have empathy with the executives who worry about them.

Now, the question is: Can you have any direct impact on Churchill's cash flow?"

"Of course I can. If they buy our MegaDoppel, we'll be taking a big chunk of their cash. That's sure an impact, especially given what our MegaDoppel costs."

"Well, Joe, if your product or service is big relative to a hospital's purchasing guidelines, it will definitely get the attention of an executive or two. But, I was thinking more in a positive sense. Does your MegaDoppel do anything positive for Churchill to help them to be more effective managing their cash flow?"

"Now that you put it that way, I guess there are a couple of things that pop into my mind. The first is that we have a very attractive leasing program that spreads out the cost of the MegaDoppel. That would allow Churchill to to use some of the cash that they would otherwise give us in an outright purchase deal for some other purposes. And, the way the MegaDoppel would impact Churchill's operations, it would cut down on some serious overtime costs they are now spending."

"Good thinking. The leasing idea does have a direct impact on the cash flow worry. It would certainly spread out the payments. Also, sometimes a lease can be turned

into an operating expense instead of a capital expense. That would free capital funds for other purchases. Which executive might be most interested in that idea?"

"Probably their Chief Financial Officer. He's the one who has to worry about getting the cash for Churchill to operate."

"Good again, Joe. See, you already know a lot about business and this idea of empathy. You have just identified a possibly good reason to make a call on the CFO at Churchill: to help the CFO to cope with the cash flow implications of acquiring something like the MegaDoppel.

Now, your competition at Super Solutions might have a comparable leasing program. If that's the case, then your leasing program may not give you a competitive advantage, but it does give you a good reason for the CFO to spend time with you. And, if the Super Solutions sales rep is as terrified of calling on executives as you are, then you may be the only one who brings this idea to the CFO, which would then give you a competitive advantage."

"Yeah, I can see that, but what about cutting out that expensive overtime?"

"That, too, Joe, is a good reason for the executives at Churchill to meet with you. The VP of Operations probably has the biggest stake in that worry since she has the budget responsibility for operations. It would also be interesting to the CFO since he worries about how the other executives are doing their jobs. In this sense, the CFO is the hospital's conscience or auditor.

A big deal with CFOs is Business Process Management. They are always looking for ways to streamline the business processes to squeeze out costs and improve productivity. Reducing overtime is definitely stream-lining.

You're getting the idea. Connect with the worries of the executive. Empathize.

Now, the situation will be different at every different hospital. But, you'll find that your products and services tend to have similar impacts at those different hospitals. You just have to learn how to recognize the worries and how to tailor your response to them."

"How do I do that?"

"Let's not get too far ahead of ourselves. We'll cover that subject in due time.

In the meantime, let's identify more typical worries for you to consider.

In the financial category, we have things like:

- *Cash flow/budget*
- *Revenue*
- *Gross profit*
- *Operating profit (EBITDA)*
- *Net profit*
- *Division or department unit profit contribution or unit cost*
- *Return on assets*
- *Return on equity*
- *Days outstanding for accounts receivables*
- *Costs*

- *Productivity*
- *Medicare and Medicaid reimbursement*
- *Patient mix*
- *Bed occupancy rate*
- *Average length of stay*

The executives constantly worry about how big each of these items is and what's the best way to control each one so as to minimize risks and maximize benefits to the hospital. If you can help them in doing any of that, then you should have a receptive audience in the executive suite to listen to what you have to offer.

This isn't a comprehensive list, but one meant to stimulate your thinking as to what your product and services might directly impact.

One other thing to note is that some of these worries are the same thing, just from a different viewpoint. For example, to reduce costs is one of the things you could do to increase profit. Also, increasing productivity is another way of reducing costs because you get more out of what you spend. You'll see similar kinds of overlap between the six categories."

"Days outstanding? Unit profit contribution? Return on assets? What are these?"

"Welcome to the world of execu-speak, Joe. These are just some of the measures and concerns that executives have and what they call them. Throughout our time together, I'll be injecting terms like these into your vocabulary. If you're going to meet with them, you better start learning their jargon.

Specifically to your question, days outstanding for accounts receivables is a measure of how long it takes for a hospital to collect the money that's due to them from their patients or the patients' insurance companies. A certain amount of time is reasonable to give patients to pay bills. If it takes too long, then the hospital loses the use of the money it hasn't yet collected. The net effect is to cost the hospital the equivalent of the interest the hospital would have earned on that money if it had collected it earlier, or to cost the hospital the interest it has to pay to borrow money to cover what it hasn't collected. Either way, it's bad news.

Now, we don't know what caused the days to be longer than desired. What do you think possible causes might be?"

"Well, just from my own experiences here at Mega Systems, I know customers might not pay if our equipment isn't working right. Or, maybe there are some missing parts when we go to install it. Or, maybe the customer is just short of cash and is pushing their problem onto us."

"All those are possibilities. It might also be that the prospect doesn't have good enough information to tell them which invoices are not being paid fast enough. Or, maybe the hospital is slow getting their invoices out in the first place. If your products and services can help the prospect in any direct way to speed up the collection of money owed to them, then you have another reason to contact their executives.

Very specific to the VP of Operations at Churchill, maybe the operations department isn't delivering the unit's expected profit contribution. That could have a big impact on the hospital and that executive's annual bonus. If you can convincingly show how you can help a unit or department meet its profit contribution objective, then that could get you the order because that executive has a big, personal win at stake...his or her bonus."

"Yeah, I can see how that would be a big personal motivator. But, what about return on assets? What's that all about?"

"Return on assets, or ROA, is another way that executives measure the performance of the business. The hospital has invested money into resources such as buildings, equipment, accounts receivables and all the other assets carried on their balance sheet. The purpose of that investment is to produce a return in the form of net profit. By comparing the amount of profit earned for the size of the investment the hospital makes, you get a measure of how productive they are in using their assets. The executives can compare their ROA to that of their competitors to see how they stack up in the industry."

"I get it. If I can increase the productivity of some assets, like helping them to be more efficient in using their clinical equipment, then I'm improving their ROA, and I have another thing to talk about with the executives."

OK, what about the other categories of worries? What's in them that I might be able to impact?"

"First, Joe, let's change the term 'worry' to something more polite and acceptable in execu-speak. Let's call

them 'drivers,' because they drive executive decision-making. It's a more positive way to refer to what an executive might be worrying about. You would say something like, 'Ms. Smith, as Vice President of Operations, it seems that the productivity of your clinical assets is a significant decision driver. Based on my preliminary research of your operations, it looks like our MegaDoppel could increase that productivity by at least 5%. Would that be of interest to you?'"

"Wow! That would just blow her away! It's Hanks, by the way. The VP of Operations at Churchill is Heather Hanks."

"Oh, OK. Hanks it is.

Let's go through the other five categories of drivers. The first was financial drivers.

Then there are marketplace drivers, things like:

- *How fast are the hospital's target markets growing?*
- *How much market share do they have in each market? How is that changing?*
- *How best to reach each market?*
- *How much does it cost to reach each market, and what return do they get from each market?*

A third set of drivers has to do with competition. Although competition is part of the marketplace, I've separated it out because it's so important to most hospitals. It includes:

- *Who are the competitors?*
- *What are they providing that competes with me? At what prices?*

- *To whom are they marketing?*
- *How are they marketing?*
- *What is their market share?*
- *Are they growing? Profitable?*
- *How do they differentiate themselves?*

The fourth category of drivers is governmental. This represents all those people who spend their working lives making rules and regulations for executives to worry about.

- *What can I or can't I do?*
- *What standards must I follow?*
- *What are the reporting requirements?*
- *Privacy requirements?*
- *Safety requirements?*

Another category is the technology used in the hospital's operations. Drivers include:

- *Am I on the leading edge of technology? Or on the 'bleeding edge'?*
- *Am I a follower? How far ahead or how far behind am I?*
- *Do I use technology as a competitive differentiator?*
- *Do I have enough technology? Too much? Is it fast enough? Big enough?*
- *Do my people know how to use it to maximum benefit?*

The last category is particularly interesting because it's more subjective to measure than the others. I call it the 'social drivers.' For example:

- *What is the morale of my people?*
- *What kind of personnel turnover do I have? Why?*

- *What is my relationship with physician groups?*
- *How do organizational changes impact us?*
- *What are the hospital politics?*

That last item, hospital politics, probably drives more decision-making than any other driver. It is very personal to the executives. It involves who is doing what to whom to advance, or who gets the big bonuses, or who gets the best office.

Joe, if you can directly help an executive to win at hospital politics, you'll have highly advanced your probability of getting the order.

Remember, people buy from people. People will buy from people who can, first, help them with their personal goals and ambitions. Hospital needs come second. In a perfect world, the two are in synch with each other. Often, the world is not entirely perfect and there is some variance that you might be able to leverage."

"Whew! What a list! How am I going to remember all of that? How am I going to find them out in the first place? And, then, you want me to decide which I can impact?"

"That's right, Joe. In terms of remembering them, I've made a list for you. But, remember, this is only a partial list. You should be looking for additional drivers that you can impact because you know your business, that is, your products and services, and how your products and services impact your prospects' businesses, or at least, you should know these things. That's an essential part of being a business representative and earning the right to call at the executive levels.

Also note that drivers can originate from inside and outside the hospital. Most governmental drivers obviously come from outside. Many of the social drivers come from inside.

As far as how to learn about the drivers of a particular executive in a particular hospital, we'll be covering that subject shortly.

For now, you should be getting a good feel for execu-speak and the drivers of executive decision-making."

"I am! I am!"

THE OTHER HALF OF AN EXECUTIVE'S JOB: MAKING DECISIONS

"Before, you said that executives do two things: worry and make their decisions about those worries. I think I understand the concept of worries...excuse me, drivers. What kind of decisions are you talking about the executives making?"

"The decision-making part of the executive's job is where his or her creativity and foresight come into play. The executives are stuck with the drivers...worries. The trick there is to recognize them and their root causes and to do that in a timely manner.

The decision-making is where the course of the hospital is determined.

It starts with the hospital's mission. A mission is what the hospital considers its business. Usually, once a year at a strategic planning session, the executives revisit their mission statement to determine if it should change because of some major impact by drivers.

It isn't often that a mission statement changes, but it happens. The telephone companies, because of deregulation, a major driver in their lives, decided to expand to be telecommunications companies instead of just telephone companies. This change opened many new business

avenues including the Internet. That change in direction also spawned many new opportunities for those who sold products and services to those telecommunication companies.

Do you know Churchill's mission?"

"I guess it's to take care of sick people. That's no big revelation that's going to help me sell them a MegaDoppel."

"Well, actually, Churchill Hospital is part of the Churchill Group. They state that the Group's mission is to 'provide high quality, cost effective health and health-related services to the people of the state.' While taking care of sick people certainly fits into that definition, it seems

to me that Churchill's business might be a little broader. For example, it includes health-related services. And, their territory is the whole state, not just this city.

Does this broader mission statement change your sales strategy in selling a MegaDoppel to Churchill? Probably not, but it does alert you to the potential that the people at Churchill think bigger than just taking care of sick people. That might be something worthwhile for you to pursue for add-on business. It's also a great topic for you to explore with an executive as to what is meant by the broader definition of Churchill's mission. That kind of question makes you look business savvy."

"That, Sely, assumes I ever get to meet a Churchill executive. Where did you see that mission statement?"

"It's on their web site and in their brochure, but more on that when we talk about researching a hospital."

"Research? I don't have time for research. My boss would kick me out of the office if he saw me sitting around doing research! Especially if the research was looking for fancy mission statements."

"Oh, Joe, you have so much to learn about business and selling. But, that's why I'm here. Just make sure your ears aren't plugged, listen carefully to what I say and how I say it, and keep an open mind.

Getting back to executive decision-making, once the mission is defined, the executives next decide how they will measure success in that mission. These measures are usually called goals or objectives. They might be things such as achieving a certain level of revenue or market share. Or, they could include a certain net profit or return on equity or return on assets.

These are generally redefined each fiscal year, although circumstances (drivers), can cause them to be modified sometime during the year."

"Yeah, I understand all that. My own company has its yearly goals and objectives. And, I'm part of a problem in reaching one of them...the revenue one...unless I can bring in Churchill. Again, I don't see how knowing Churchill's goals or objectives is going to help me sell a MegaDoppel to them."

"What we are doing, Joe, is building your understanding of the general business picture at your prospect. First, you try to understand the drivers that you might be able to directly impact. Next, you get a broad framework of the prospect's business by understanding the mission and their overall goals and objectives. It's the next decision-making piece where you can really play.

But, before we talk about that, you should realize that just as a hospital has a mission, goals and objectives, so too do the major departments of the hospital. These lower level missions, goals and objectives should fully support the overall hospital's corresponding items. The sum total of all the department plans should fully enable the hospital's plan.

If you are particularly observant, you might occasionally run across a situation where a department's goals or objectives might actually be misaligned to the overall hospital plan. That's a sure red flag for you to talk about with the head of the department...not in a threatening way, but in an inquisitive, helpful way.

For example, if you said, 'I notice that your objective this year in your department is to cut costs, while the rest of the hospital is talking about expanding their operations to go after new markets. Isn't your objective out of step with the hospital?' The department head might be offended by your statement as saying he or she was rowing in the wrong direction.

Instead, if you said, 'As I understand it, a major objective of your department this year is to cut costs. How will this play into the hospitals broader plans to expand into new markets?' Now, you aren't questioning the validity of the logic. Rather, you are seeking to understand how the pieces fit together."

"You sure have a way with words, Sely."

"And, by the time we finish, Joe, so will you. It's just good business common sense.

The point of all this so far is that you should be aware of the hospital's big picture so that it helps you to talk about the overall business and about how you might impact that business.

Which gets us to the next point. Once the goals and objectives are set, then the executives decide on the major strategies the hospital will use to achieve those goals and objectives. They also identify what absolutely must happen in order for those strategies to succeed. These must-happen actions are called 'critical success factors' or CSFs.

Now, it's usually at the strategy and critical success factor level of executive decision-making where you can have the most direct impact. You should identify which strategies and which CSFs your products and services can enable or enhance. There is where you want to focus your selling efforts and where you have the reason to meet with the appropriate executives responsible for those strategies and CSFs. If you really can impact some part of those strategies and CSFs in a significant way, they need to meet with you."

"I get it. At Churchill, there was a lot of talk about increasing productivity in operations. That must be a big executive strategy if all the troops are talking about it. As you said before, the executives' bonuses are probably wrapped around increasing productivity."

"Right. Strategies from the top cause a lot of energy down below, especially when the executives have a big personal stake in the results. But sometimes, the strategies get warped and misinterpreted as they filter down. That's one of the main reasons for you to spend some quality time with executives to hear, first-hand, what they want to achieve and how they see it happening."

"OK, let me see if I have this down right. I start with drivers, the things executives worry about. I'm looking for things that I can impact with my products and services. Then, I take a look at the prospect's mission, goals, objectives, strategies and critical success factors. Again, I'm looking for things I can impact. Do I have it right?"

"Yes, you have it right. But remember, your impact must be direct. Otherwise, people can discount what you

have to offer. If you can demonstrate or prove a direct connection that significantly impacts a driver or a strategy or a CSF, they will sit up and take notice."

"Right. I understand. Now, you've been dancing around this all day: Where do I learn all these things about my prospect? Do I have to go to the executives to learn them?"

I would never make a critical buying decision that will have a major impact on my enterprise without meeting with the salesperson.

Vice President, Operations
Financial Investment
Company

"The executives are certainly the best source. But, unless you're very lucky, they aren't likely to entertain a meeting with you to educate you on their business. As one executive I know says, 'There is nothing in my compensation plan that rewards me for educating sales reps.'

So, going to an executive with a blank pad asking questions like, 'What are you worrying about?' or 'What are your goals and objectives this year?' is probably not going to earn you much respect and input.

What you have to do is homework...research, just like back in school. Fortunately, there's plenty of information available. That's the subject of our next lesson: how to develop an initial understanding of your prospect's business."

REVIEW KEY POINTS

1. People buy from people. Your best strategy to win their support is empathy. See the world from their point of view. Look for ways to make them successful and to make their hospital successful. But, making them *personally* successful is far more important.

2. Look for executive drivers (worries) that you can *directly* impact. Add your own observations to these lists:

   ### Financial drivers:
   - Cash flow/budget
   - Revenue/sales
   - Gross profit
   - Operating profit (EBITDA)
   - Net profit
   - Division or department unit profit contribution or unit cost
   - Return on assets
   - Return on equity
   - Days outstanding for accounts receivables
   - Costs
   - Productivity
   - Medicare and Medicaid reimbursement
   - Patient mix
   - Bed occupancy rate
   - Average length of stay

   _____

   _____

   _____

Marketplace drivers:

- Growth of the marketplace
- Growth of market share
- How best to reach the marketplace
- Cost to reach the marketplace

Competitive drivers:

- Who are the competitors?
- What are they providing that competes with me? At what prices?
- To whom are they marketing?
- How are they marketing?
- What is their market share?
- Are they growing? Profitable?
- How do they differentiate themselves?

Regulatory drivers:

- What can I or can't I do?
- What standards must I follow?
- What are the reporting requirements?
- Privacy requirements?
- Safety requirements?

Technology drivers:

- Am I on the leading edge of technology? Or on the 'bleeding edge'?
- Am I a follower? How far ahead or how far behind?
- Do I use technology as a competitive differentiator?
- Do I have enough technology? Too much? Fast enough? Big enough?
- Do my people know how to use it to maximum benefit?

_____

_____

_____

Social drivers:

- What is the morale of my people?
- What kind of personnel turnover do I have? Why?
- What is my relationship with physician groups?
- How do organizational changes impact us?
- What are the hospital politics?

_____

_____

_____

3. Understand the prospect's overall business and where you can directly impact their strategies and critical success factors:

- *Mission* – what the hospital does for a business
- *Goals/Objectives* – the way the executives measure success in the business
- *Strategies* – how the executives expect to achieve their goals and objectives
- *Critical Success Factors* – what must go right or the hospital will fail in some or all of their goals and objectives

DISCUSSION TOPICS

1. Pick one or two of the executives in your own company. What drivers are worrying them?

2. For your own company, what are... ?

- Mission statement
- Goals and objectives
- Major strategies
- Critical success factors

3. Pick one of your prospects with whom you have been dealing for a while. What do you think are their... ?

- Mission statement
- Goals and objectives
- Major strategies
- Critical success factors

DON'T BE INTIMIDATED!

CHAPTER 3:
DO YOUR HOMEWORK

WHY DO THE WORK?

"**Y**ou know, Sely, I've already got more to do than I have the time to do it. Now, you want to add homework? I don't have time for that."

A rep had better know my business if he gets a meeting with me. I can't tell you how many terrible and short meetings that I have had with sales reps who don't know my business.

CEO
Computer Software Company

"*Joe, I can certainly appreciate how busy you are. No one is holding a gun to your head demanding that you make sales calls to executives. As I said before, there are no black and whites in selling. The objectives are how to minimize risks and maximize results.*

There are times in a sales situation when calling on an executive can make a big difference. But, if you are confident you don't need that strategy, then, I agree, let's forget it. By the way, when did you say that Churchill order would be closed?"

"That was a dirty blow! So, maybe a call on the VP of Operations might help me at Churchill. What kind of homework are you talking about? And, why can't I just go call on her without wasting a lot of time doing research?"

"Again, Joe, no black and whites. If you want to take the risk of calling on her without having any background on her or her needs, then go right ahead. It could very well work. I wouldn't do it, but I'm not you. I prefer to show executives that I'm interested enough in them and their business that I took the time and effort to do some preparation. I consider it a show of respect for them and their time. In my experience, it's appreciated.

But, maybe the VP of Operations at Churchill doesn't care about things like that. Go try."

"Don't get so holier-than-thou. Besides, I already know a lot about the operational needs at Churchill. What do you think I've been doing over there these last two months?"

I would never do business with a company that sends an uninformed salesperson to me.

CEO
Financial Institution

You know what I hate is salespeople who call me with no relevant business scenario for me, but want to play golf or fly me to some fancy resort. They obviously don't understand my business.

President
Aluminum Window
Manufacturer

"Whatever it was, it doesn't look like it was enough, hmmm? If I remember correctly, it was your lamenting about losing that big sale that brought me into your consciousness in the first place."

"Is that what you call this inquisition...into my consciousness?"

"Joe, it's very possible that you already know enough about Ms. Hanks' drivers, strategies and critical suc-

44

cess factors to make a productive call on her. Let's just go through the exercise to make sure. Let's minimize the risks. OK?

As I said, the best place to learn this information is directly from the executive's mouth. But, the challenge is to jump-start the conversation by gaining the executive's interest and respect so that he or she will spend the time to educate you. Walking in with a blank sheet is very dangerous and really unnecessary. The information is usually easily available. Why take the risk?"

It is so disappointing when a sales rep calls on me unprepared about my business, especially if it is something strategic. It is not so important that they know or have come from the airline industry, but they had better know what my business is and how their solution is going to solve my specific problems. When they come to me uneducated about that, it is usually a very brief meeting that is embarrassing for the salesperson.

Vice President, Marketing
Airline

"Why can't I get what I need just from talking with the people on the selection committee? Then, I don't have to spend a lot of time doing research."

"First, we are not talking about a lot of time. We are talking about an hour or so.

Second, the information you get about an executive and that executive's interests is going to be biased by the person giving you that information. Sometimes, the bias is very small and the information is good enough to make the call. But, it's dangerous to assume so. It's better to broaden your sources. I would still do the research to double check.

It's also possible you might start a sales campaign with an executive prior to speaking with anyone else. A little later, we'll talk about the timing of executive calls. You'll see that starting with an executive is sometimes a dynamite strategy."

"OK, so an hour isn't that much time, but it sure adds up if I have to do it for every one of my accounts. I'll be a permanent researcher! That sure isn't going to make my boss happy in meeting my quota. Maybe he'll give me commission on the beauty of my research!"

"Boy, are you a whiner!"

"What did you say? I didn't hear that."

"Oh, I just said, I want to make you a winner.

Look, no one said you had to spend this level of effort with every prospect. In many cases, you may decide you don't need to meet an executive. The sales situation could be very straightforward, just requiring a technical and pricing response from you.

That's one of the exciting aspects of selling. You get to set the strategy for every opportunity. Selling is a thinking person's game. As long as you make more good choices than bad and meet your own company's expectations in terms of orders and revenue, then you're labeled a successful salesperson.

Of course, I'm trying to help you be a successful business representative. Knowing your prospect and knowing the needs and interests of all the key people at the hospital, including those executives relevant to your products and services, are all part of becoming a trusted advisor to your prospect. That's another, more meaningful definition of a business representative: a trusted advisor.

Now, here is where we are in this great debate. You can take the risk of going into an executive meeting with a blank page, or you can do some homework ahead of time to show you care enough to spend the effort. You can get the prerequisite information from others at the prospect or even outside the prospect. But, that comes with built-in biases. It's still useful to have that input. If nothing else, it will eventually show how distorted the executive messages might get in that particular organization."

YOU ARE AN EXPERT

"OK, Sely, you have me sufficiently convinced that it is a good idea to do homework...some of the time. Now, let's get more specific about this homework. Just what does it involve?"

"The mechanics are pretty easy. The hard part is developing a 'consultative eye' as you scan the information. You just want to pick out those things that will help you to help your prospect. You don't want a data-overload with lots of relatively useless information.

This brings up another one of those critical points for you to understand...a CSF for you. You don't have to be an expert in your prospect's business. You have to be an expert in how you might impact the prospect's business.

Your boss and your prospects expect you to be an expert in your business and how your business will impact the prospects. This knowledge and attitude are critical to you. It's what gives you the right to demand to meet anyone at a prospect whom you can help. They need you. They need to talk with you to understand how you can provide that help.

I'm reminded of the cartoon that shows a medieval king, short sword in hand, ready to charge off to meet the enemy with his poorly armed troops. He's telling a messenger, 'Tell the salesman to come back later. I'm busy.' Then, we see the salesman getting a machine gun ready for a demonstration to the king.

Tell the salesman to come back later, I'm busy.

I wonder how many executives have missed opportunities because they were too busy to see salespeople. I don't blame the executives. I blame the salespeople for not earning the right to get in the door or for not making the best use of the executive's time once they do get in. All of which we'll be talking about."

"I like that. I *am* an expert in what we do. I know the MegaDoppel inside and out. I must confess that I have some things to learn about how it works best in some of my prospects' businesses, but, on the whole, I have a pretty good idea of how it can help most of my prospects.

You're right, Sely. They *do* need me. I can make them successful. By George, I'm going to demand those meetings!"

"Joe, let's take it a little slower. There is a less risky way to make those demands.

First, let's get you the information you need to provide the punch behind the demand."

WHAT TO LOOK FOR

"I bet I know one of the places you're going to suggest. The hospital's web site, right?"

"Yep, a hospital's web site is probably the first and best place to go. In the case of Churchill, it's the Churchill Group web site that covers the three hospitals in the Group.

What do you think you should look at on the site?"

"Well, based on what we talked about, I would look at the section that talks about the hospital"

"Right, again. It's usually a link on the home page that's called 'About Us' or something like that. In the 'About Us' section, there will often be a mission statement. If there isn't an explicit mission statement, then there is typically a short description of the hospital, its business, even some history."

I see sales reps all of the time. I often will meet with new companies as long as the proposition makes sense to me. It is how I stay current with what is new and where the market is headed.

Vice President, Marketing
Airline

"I've also seen a section on the hospital's officers and board of directors."

"Yes, that's a particularly important one for you to look at if you plan on visiting any executives at the hospital. If you're lucky, there will be biographies describing the background and current job for each executive you want to meet.

I don't think you'll have much trouble deciding which executives are important to you. Their titles usually give you that direction. You want to consider meeting the executives whose departments or operations can directly benefit from your products and services.

Most hospitals will also have a 'news' or 'press release' section on their 'About Us' page. You should definitely skim-read the titles of any news and press releases to see if there is something that relates to what you will be doing with the hospital. I like to go back six months if it's my first time researching a hospital. I might even go back twelve months if I know little about them."

"How will I know that from skim-reading titles?"

"It's not hard. It just takes a little practice to develop an eye for useful information.

For example, is there a press release about a new executive in charge of an area you will impact? A new executive usually means change. And, since you are an agent of change, there might be a very receptive interest on the part of this executive and his or her subordinates to consider what you have to say."

I use sales folks as research to learn what other companies are experiencing in the market.

CEO
Computer Software Company

Salespeople who hide the fact that they don't know my business fail in short order. On the other hand, I don't expect the salespeople to be CIOs, and frankly, I respect those who don't try to be.

CIO
Retailer

"Oh, I like that: an agent of change."

"Another example might be a press release about the opening or closing of a facility where your product or service might be useful. Again, this implies change. Change is a good omen for you, because people are more open to considering something new or different when there already is a major change in process. They have already been shaken from their reluctance to change.

A new service introduction or a move into a new market or geography are more changes that might be openings for you. Mergers and acquisitions can be interest-

ing, especially if the acquired or merged hospital is already a customer of your company.

Put yourself into their shoes...empathize...how can you help them to achieve whatever they are trying to achieve with the change. Can you make it easier? Faster? More productive? How can you make the people heroes to the CEO and to themselves by leveraging your products and services to accomplish the change?"

"I like that, too. I'm a hero-maker! Plus an agent of change. And a trusted advisor. Wait until my boss hears me spouting this stuff.

Tell me more. This is getting good!"

A GOLDMINE OF INFORMATION:
THE CEO'S LETTER

"An important part for you to read is the letter from the CEO, usually written at the beginning or end of the fiscal year. It often contains a rich assortment of useful information for you, specifically, drivers, strategies and critical success factors.

To take this idea out of the theoretical, let's take a look at the CEO's letter on Churchill Group's web site. The focus you should have as you read the letter is what are drivers, strategies and critical success factors that you can impact by selling them a MegaDoppel. Also, be alert to other intelligence useful for your sales campaign.

Just underline and mark comments in the margins of the letter. I'm going to ask our audience to do the same."

"Audience? What audience?"

"Don't worry about it, Joe. Just read the letter and make your notations."

CHURCHILL
HOSPITAL GROUP

LETTER FROM THE C. E. O.

Year in Review

Last year was a difficult year for our Group. But, despite the challenges, we achieved a respectable performance. It is a testament to our dedicated and capable 3,500 employees that we persevered and made progress in such an unsettled economic environment.

Our overall revenue was flat comparing last year with the previous year. Revenues last year were $750 million, representing less than 1% growth. Considering the soft economy's impact on our investment portfolio and the reductions in Medicare and Medicaid reimbursement rates, this was actually a significant achievement.

The good news is that we were profitable for the year. This profit was achieved through a combination of two, new, highly successful, service offerings and two, cost-containment initiatives implemented during the year: "Squeeze It Out" and "Raise the Bar."

The new services, Center for Women's Health and Center for Digestive Disorders, have had immediate acceptance and impact across our service areas.

The first cost-containment initiative, "Squeeze It Out," refers to a cost-cutting campaign driven from the bottom up. We asked our employees to look for places to eliminate unnecessary and redundant costs. They responded with enthusiasm and vigor.

The second cost-containment campaign, initiated in the second half of the fiscal year, was also employee-driven. During the cost cutting, many suggestions were made to change processes to increase productivity. So, we capitalized on this creativity by building it into a campaign.

As a result of these four efforts, aimed at new revenue and both sides of the cost equation, our operating margins have improved by 15%. We rewarded these efforts by sharing the success in the form of bonuses for ideas that produced results. We were also able to keep our staff intact with no layoffs. We intend to continue all of these programs into our new year.

Services to the Community

Churchill Group is a full-service care provider with in-patient and out-patient programs located in Capitol City, Centralia and, through our recent merger with Adelphia Hospital, in Monroe. Our census last year across all our facilities was:

```
Annual inpatient admissions:    Acute  54,000
Annual inpatient days:          Acute 210,000
Annual emergency visits:              150,000
Annual outpatient visits:              35,000
Total beds (in-patient and out-patient):   650
   (Capitol City - 400; Centralia - 150;
   Monroe - 100)
Affiliated physicians:                    930
```

We are particularly proud of our Centers of Excellence in heart programs, oncology, sports medicine, and the new centers in women's health and digestive disorders.

We are accredited by the Joint Commission on Accreditation of Healthcare Organizations (JCAHO).

Strategies to Succeed

We have worked hard to achieve our strong market positions in our principal service areas and our Centers of Excellence. A major emphasis in this new year is to grow our revenue and our census across all of our sectors by new and expanded services and by acquisition. We look to attract more affiliated physicians and more patients through these strategies.

To this end, we have recently announced our intent to acquire Miramar Hospital, which specializes in diabetes and endocrine care. Miramar principally serves the Macon City region. This acquisition should be finalized shortly. The addition of this 120-bed hospital will allow us to offer more specialized care to our communities across the state and to bring our existing capabilities to the people of Macon City. We continue to examine other opportunities to expand through acquisition.

As mentioned previously, we will continue our two programs to squeeze cost and improve productivity. Accordingly, to increase the effectiveness of our efforts, we will introduce more state-of-the-art technology into our processes. We need to continue making significant advances to keep our costs low to provide quality service at a reasonable price.

We have affiliated with the Allison School of Medicine of the State University in Capitol City to provide an excellent teaching environment for medical students and to avail ourselves of the excellent medical research being done at that school. To lead our affiliation, we have added Dr. Samuel Medicus to our medical staff. Dr. Medicus is a well-known innovator in cardiology. We should soon see the impact of his efforts in enhanced modalities of care for our patients.

We will add emphasis to delivering the best in medical care. To aid us in that effort, we are adopting the six sigma quality initiative that has proven to be very successful in many types of businesses and service organizations.

Management Team

In addition to Dr. Medicus, Ms. Heather Hanks has joined Churchill as our new Vice President of Operations. In this position, she is responsible for all the services and quality programs at Churchill. She replaces Ed Luft who has retired. We wish Ed all the best for a well-earned time of ease.

We have in place a highly talented and innovative leadership team, who, together with our staff and affiliated physicians who share those same qualities, will deliver exceptional quality of care and accelerate our growth across the state.

In Conclusion

This coming year is a big year for Churchill Group. We intend to fully live up to the expectations of all our constituencies, especially the patients we serve. We have a reputation for innovation in what we do and how we do it. I look forward to writing you next year with a report that I strongly expect will highlight the advancement of Churchill in broadened services and service areas.

Sincerely,

Max Profitt

Max Profitt
Chairman and CEO

"Joe, what do you think of what you just read?"

"Well, Mr. Profitt certainly sounds like a confident man. It looks like he's placing his job on the line, almost promising a big increase in business at Churchill."

"Yes, I would agree that he has certainly taken a strong stand on bettering performance. How do you think he's going to make it happen?"

"I guess you're asking me to identify the key strategies and critical success factors for Churchill in the coming year. I've underlined them in my copy of the letter. I also underlined what I think are the drivers that are impacting the decision-making at Churchill."

"OK, share some of that with me."

"Drivers first. Last year wasn't a great revenue year for Churchill. Revenues were flat. But they did increase their profits. That means that there's more cash to work with.

It appears that two other drivers are the soft economy's impact on their investment income and reduced payment rates by Medicare and Medicaid.

Their two new Centers of Excellence, women's health and digestive disorders, were successes. They appear to have given Churchill some needed revenue to cover their shortfall elsewhere.

They mentioned they are accredited by JCAHO. I think they may have a quality problem somewhere, especially given that bit about adopting a six sigma quality initiative.

Did I get all the drivers?"

"Joe, it isn't important whether or not you got all the drivers. What is important is that you have a better understanding of what is driving the executive decision-making at Churchill.

That interpretation about quality being a problem is intriguing. Very insightful of you to pick that up. Even if quality isn't a problem, it certainly seems important enough for Churchill to spend some new effort on it.

You should realize that this letter is very carefully crafted and re-crafted. The CEO can't lie or exaggerate. He or she has to present the status of the hospital realistically, or else some government agency might have something to say about deliberately misleading the public.

I expect you now have a number of interesting questions that you could ask those executives that will further draw out possible needs for your products and services. Care to give me a couple?"

"Yeah. I'd like to ask the new VP of Operations what changes she plans to make to increase quality in their operations. Our MegaDoppel can have a big impact on quality, especially in workflow.

If I see the VP of Business Development, I'd like to hear what he thinks are the competitive differentiators for Churchill in their service areas. That would give me clues as to where to emphasize what we can do to enhance their competitive differentiation."

"Joe, those are excellent questions at the executive level. Here are a couple more that are suggested by the drivers you listed.

In light of the cuts in Medicare and Medicaid reimbursement rates that Churchill experienced last year, an interesting question for the operations executive is what strategies do they intend to pursue to eliminate or minimize costs while still providing the required service levels to patients. Or, maybe they will look to change their patient mix or their mix of in-patient and out-patient facilities.

Let's turn to strategies and critical success factors. What did you learn?"

"As useful as it was to think about the drivers, the strategies are really what got me excited.

First, they are continuing to squeeze out costs and increase productivity. They plan to increase the use of technology in doing that. That's music to my ears and money in my pocket! Here comes Joe and his MegaDoppel!

But, there's more that I didn't have any idea about until I read the letter.

They are planning big time growth of market share in all their services and service areas. They also imply they are going to add new Centers of Excellence. And, they seem to understand that they need new processes to achieve that growth.

They're buying hospitals like Adelphia and Miramar. That means more opportunities for me.

They have a new cardiology guru who is going to be leading their affiliation with State University. Teaching hospitals are great prospects for MegaDoppels.

The VP of Operations is new. I didn't know that. No doubt, she's going to make changes. Change equals opportunity in my business, right?

I already mentioned quality. That's a big area for me to address with the MegaDoppel.

As far as critical success factors, I would have to say cost cutting and productivity increases and quality are probably very critical to Churchill.

How did I do?"

"Again, Joe, there's no score here. The idea is for you to better understand the hospital and the issues and strategies of the executives so that you can walk in with smart questions instead of a blank page.

All your interpretations appear on the money.

Notice that there was no specific statement of what was critical to Churchill. You made that inference based on the strategies and the emphases placed in the letter.

Take a look at the letter I marked up. Compare your letter to mine. You might have more, less or different items highlighted, because you were reading it from the viewpoint of your particular products and services."

CHURCHILL
HOSPITAL GROUP

LETTER FROM THE C.E.O.

Year in Review

Driver Last year was a difficult year for our Group. But, despite the challenges, we achieved a respectable per- *Driver* formance. It is a testament to our dedicated and capable *Intel-ligence* 3,500 employees that we persevered and made progress in such an unsettled economic environment. *Driver*

Driver Our overall revenue was flat comparing last year with the previous year. Revenues last year were $750 mil- *Intel-ligence* lion, representing less than 1% growth. Considering the soft economy's impact on our investment portfolio *Drivers* and the reductions in Medicare and Medicaid reimbursement rates, this was actually a significant achievement.

The good news is that we were profitable for the year. *Driver* This profit was achieved through a combination of two new, highly successful, service offerings and two cost-containment initiatives implemented during the year: "Squeeze It Out" and "Raise the Bar." *Strategies*

Strategy The new services, Center for Women's Health and Center for Digestive Disorders, have had immediate acceptance and impact across our service areas.

The first cost-containment initiative, "Squeeze It Out," refers to a cost-cutting campaign driven from the bottom up. We asked our employees to look for places to eliminate unnecessary and redundant costs. They responded with enthusiasm and vigor.

The second cost-containment campaign, initiated in the second half of the fiscal year, was also employee-

62

driven. During the cost cutting, many suggestions were made to change processes to increase productivity. So, we capitalized on this creativity by building it into a campaign.

As a result of these four efforts, aimed at new revenue and both sides of the cost equation, our operating *Driver* margins have improved by 15%. We rewarded these efforts by sharing the success in the form of bonuses for ideas that produced results. We were also able to *Intelligence* keep our staff intact with no layoffs. We intend to continue all of these programs into our new year. *Strategy*

Services to the Community

Churchill Group is a full-service care provider with in-patient and out-patient programs located in Capitol City, Centralia and, through our recent merger with Adelphia Hospital, in Monroe. Our census last year across all our facilities was:

```
Annual inpatient admissions:     Acute   54,000
Annual inpatient days:           Acute  210,000
Annual emergency visits:                150,000
Annual outpatient visits:                35,000   Intelligence
Total beds (in-patient and out-patient):   650
   (Capitol City - 400; Centralia - 150;
   Monroe - 100)
Affiliated physicians:                      930
```

We are particularly proud of our Centers of Excellence in heart programs, oncology, sports medicine, and the new centers in women's health and digestive disorders. *Intelligence*

We are accredited by the Joint Commission on Accreditation of Healthcare Organizations (JCAHO). *Intelligence*

Strategies to Succeed

Objective & Strategies

We have worked hard to achieve our strong market positions in our principal service areas and our Centers of Excellence. A major emphasis in this new year is to grow our revenue and our census across all of our sectors by new and expanded services and by acquisition. We look to attract more affiliated physicians and more patients through these strategies.

Strategy

Intelligence
To this end, we have recently announced our intent to acquire Miramar Hospital, which specializes in diabetes and endocrine care. Miramar principally serves the Macon City region. This acquisition should be finalized shortly. The addition of this 120-bed hospital will *Intelligence* allow us to offer more specialized care to our communities across the state and to bring our existing capabilities to the people of Macon City. We continue to examine other opportunities to expand through acquisition. *Strategy*

Strategies & (CSFs)

As mentioned previously, we will continue our two programs to squeeze cost and improve productivity. Accordingly, to increase the effectiveness of our efforts, we will introduce more state-of-the-art technology into our processes. We need to continue making signifi-*Strategy* cant advances to keep our costs low to provide quality service at a reasonable price.

Strategy

We have affiliated with the Allison School of Medicine of State University in Capitol City to provide an excellent teaching environment for medical students and to avail ourselves of the excellent medical research being done at that school. To lead our affiliation, we have *Strategy* added Dr. Samuel Medicus to our medical staff. Dr. Medicus is a well-known innovator in cardiology. We should soon see the impact of his efforts in enhanced modalities of care for our patients.

Objective

We will add emphasis to delivering the best in medical care. To aid us in that effort, we are adopting the six sigma quality initiative that has proven to be very successful in many types of businesses and service organizations.

Strategy & (CSF)

Management Team

Strategy

In addition to Dr. Medicus, Ms. Heather Hanks has joined Churchill as our new Vice President of Operations. In this position, she is responsible for all the services and quality programs at Churchill. She replaces Ed Luft who has retired. We wish Ed all the best for a well-earned time of ease.

We have in place a highly talented and innovative leadership team, who, together with our staff and affiliated physicians who share those same qualities, will deliver exceptional quality of care and accelerate our growth across the state.

Objective

In Conclusion

This coming year is a big year for Churchill Group. We intend to fully live up to the expectations of all our constituencies, especially the patients we serve. We have a reputation for innovation in what we do and how we do it. I look forward to writing you next year with a report that I strongly expect will highlight the advancement of Churchill in broadened services and service areas.

Sincerely,

Max Profitt

Max Profitt
Chairman and CEO

HOW TO USE THIS STRATEGIC INFORMATION

"So, Joe, what you mainly get from the CEO's letter to the shareholders are drivers and strategies. Sometimes, the letter will contain specific goals or objectives. And, you can usually infer some of the critical success factors if they are not explicitly described.

Again, keep in mind how carefully crafted this letter is. It contains the major things that the hospital's executives want to make clear to the multiple audiences for the letter: patients, staff, physician groups, suppliers, benefactors, government and accreditation agencies, even competitors. It's powerful information. It quickly generates a series of questions and ideas as to where your products and services might fit.

I said before, that it's not a good idea to walk into an executive's office and start asking very broad questions like, 'What are the issues you are facing?' or 'What are your goals and strategies for this year?' or 'What is critical to your success this year?'

While these are certainly strategic questions for an executive, he or she just doesn't have the time to educate you on such a broad basis, even if the executive did know you and had confidence and trust in you. Of course, in a first-time meeting, the probability of the executive having such confidence and trust is very low.

So, therein lies the power of the research. It breaks the blank page by giving you opening comments to show you have done the homework and understand some of the impact of what you have learned. From there, you

66

can launch into more specific and meaningful questions which furthers your business savvy in the mind of the executive."

"Yeah, Sely, I have to admit, reading that letter certainly gave me a lot more understanding of Churchill and showed me more opportunities and justification potential for my MegaDoppel. It definitely wasn't a waste of time."

"It didn't take long, did it?"

"No, it was pretty fast to do.

OK, I'm sold. I'll read the CEO's letter for my important accounts. It'll give me good stuff to show them how smart I am, even with the lower levels."

"Just so you aren't too smart, there is a caution in using this information."

"I knew it. I knew it. It was too easy to be true. Now there's a big catch."

"Not so big, but definitely a catch. Not all hospital CEOs write leters as detailed as the one we just read from Churchill. In some cases, you won't find a letter at all. That doesn't mean that there's no useful information to research in these cases. It just means that there is less of it.

Sometimes, a hospital is a member of a group, as in the case of Churchill Hospital which is the flagship of the Churchill Group, and you will find more useful information researching the group's web site in the same way as you would research a particular hospital's site.

You should do this additional research even if there's a lot of information on the web site of the particular hospital in which you are interested. The group web site will provide you with a higher level of strategic information that helps define the strategies of the individual hospitals in the group. At a minimum, you could ask an executive how a particular group level strategy impacts the strategies of the hospital. That's a good question that can stimulate very good sales information for you.

Also, keep in mind that any CEO letter is written at a given time, usually at the end of the fiscal year or close to the beginning of the new fiscal year. By the time you read it, it could be as much as a year old. Things change, even at the strategic level. Some of the information in the letter could no longer be relevant or correct."

"So now, you're telling me I'll look stupid spouting off about stuff that isn't relevant anymore. That will sure build confidence and trust in me real fast, won't it?"

"You can still use the information. Just don't make declarative statements. Hedge your statements more as questions than assumptions. For example, don't say, 'I see from your CEO's letter on your web site that you are under some very tough cost pressures. What are you doing to combat that pressure?'

Instead, say, 'From reading your CEO's letter on your web site, it seems that Churchill might be under some tough cost pressures. Is that still the case?' If the executive says it is still the case, then you can ask your next question, 'What are you doing to combat those pressures?'

See what I mean? Discount your knowledge. Give the executive an opportunity to confirm or correct your understanding. That way, you avoid looking out of date.

Keep this in mind in all your research. It's dated and may have changed by the time you use it."

"OK, I can see how to do that. But, it seems to me the older the information, the less useful."

"In general, that's true. The good news is that hospitals often publish newsletters and issue press releases that provide updates to this kind of information. If the hospital is important enough to you, you can usually subscribe to their web distribution list or make it a habit to check their web site periodically, say once a month. Skim-reading that information helps to keep your knowledge current.

By the way, Joe, when you meet with an executive and are reviewing the information you've gathered, it's a good idea to use the actual printouts of the information with your marks and underlines. It shows the executive that you really have done some homework.

There are a few more points to glean from the CEO's letter and the web site.

One thing to look for is any management change in an area of the hospital which would likely use your products and services. A change in management usually means a change in processes. Typically, a new executive has his or her own ideas as to what should be done and how. They aren't necessarily tied to the old ways of doing things, especially if the person has been brought in from outside the hospital. They are open to new ideas to make things better. They might even have been brought into the job to clean up a mess left by the predecessor.

As a business representative and advisor, you are an agent of enabling successful change to the extent that your products and services impact that change."

"Yeah. At Churchill, there's the new VP of Operations, Heather Hanks. I didn't realize she was so new. She probably has a whole list of changes to make Churchill more cost-efficient and to improve quality."

"Very possibly. Now, you have good ammunition to make a productive and impressive visit to her.

Another thing to look for are mergers and acquisitions. You already commented on Churchill's acquisition of Miramar possibly opening a new avenue of opportunity.

Consolidation or expansion of locations or departments also implies big changes and new issues to resolve.

Also be alert to other tidbits of information that could eventually be useful in your sales campaign. In the Churchill report, the CEO thanked his 3,500 employees. You also learned census information. These might be factors that impact how your products and services might be useful to the hospital."

"How do I know what stuff to look for?"

"Some of it is obvious based on what your products and services can do. Some of it comes with experi-

ence. You start with the obvious and begin to develop a nose for tidbits.

To summarize what we've talked about here, you are trying to determine where a hospital is going and how it's getting there. You are very interested in the pains and the gaps in their efforts. If you can relieve those pains and fill those gaps, then they need you. You're the doctor, the specialist. If you can do that better than your competition and at a price the prospect is willing to pay, then you get the order."

I can't tell you how many salespeople whom I trusted and liked then wasted my time, because they did not understand my business drivers. Frankly, I don't have time to teach them. There is no excuse for a sales rep who has an opportunity to sell to me, the CEO of a multibillion-dollar enterprise, to blow it because they are unprepared. I usually politely dismiss myself with an unexpected meeting that has come up.

CEO
Hospital

"Now, I'm a doctor! Trusted advisor, agent of change, hero-maker. I don't know if I can fit all these titles on my business card."

"I'll give you a very convenient checklist to help you to develop your nose for business intelligence. After doing it for a short time, it will become habit."

"Umm, easy for you to say."

MORE BUSINESS INTELLIGENCE

"Before we leave the subject of the web site, there are a couple of additional things you might quickly look for.

There is often a hospital mission statement. However it's worded, that's the way they think of themselves and the business they are in.

In Churchill's case, they say they provide 'high quality, cost effective health and health-related services to the people of the state.' Does this mean anything special to you, Joe?"

"I don't know. It certainly means it's a hospital. They talk about high quality, which is perfect for my MegaDoppel. I don't know why they used such fancy words to describe a hospital."

"I suspect, Joe, that they are defining their business broadly enough to incorporate other services than just those usually associated with a general hospital. It does generate a nice question to ask: 'What additional services are you pursuing beyond those of a general hospital?' That could produce another avenue of opportunity for you to pursue.

They also think of themselves as bigger than just this one city. They look at the entire state as their service area. Again, this raises questions about where they are focusing on expanding.

It's useful to quickly skim the other sections of the web site. Sometimes useful tidbits come out of that. Be alert to any drivers, strategies, critical success factors and big change."

"What about the financial stuff? That scares me."

"Some sales reps are very comfortable reading and interpreting the financials. That's to their added benefit.

It's not my intent in working with you to make you a financial analyst. I want to make this effort very easy and logical for you. So, unless you are already skilled at reading and interpreting the financial numbers, it's best you just stick with the things I'm showing you. I'll give some brief insight into some of the more obvious numbers as we go."

I expect the salesperson to be literate in my business, and they had better be relevant to the problem I am trying to solve.

Chief Procurement Officer
Defense Contractor

"Just as well with me. I prefer to have as little to do with that stuff as I can. If I wanted to be a numbers guy, I would have been a mathematician or accountant. The only numbers I care about in this job are my quota and my commissions."

"To help make the numbers meaningful, you look for three things: size, trend, comparisons.

By size, I mean: are the numbers big enough to get your attention? For example, Churchill has revenues of $750 million. At that size, they're probably big enough in your territory to get your attention."

"Actually, a hospital as small as $50 million in revenue could be a good prospect for a MegaDoppel."

"See. You already understand the concept of size.

Trend is another obvious indicator in analyzing numbers. What would you say is the trend at Churchill?"

"Well, revenues look like they are up a little bit and they are profitable. So, the trend is positive, but it's not good enough for Mr. Profitt. They expect this year to be much better."

"So, how does that influence your thinking about Churchill?"

"Well, they aren't desperate, but they probably aren't throwing money around like there's no tomorrow. I would say that they would be quite cautious in how they make investments, but they are willing to take a look and spend where it makes sense. I already know that they are tough negotiators on price and that their CFO requires a strong return on investment business case to approve a capital purchase."

"Good, that's how to interpret the trends.

Lastly, there are comparisons. You already mentioned one comparison: last year's revenues compared to the previous year. Those also give us a trend.

But, there are other comparisons. We talked about one earlier: return on assets, where we compare net profit to total assets. You just mentioned one: return on investment, where we compare the return in profit from an investment in your MegaDoppel to the cost of the MegaDoppel. These comparisons are usually expressed as ratios.

There is another form of comparison. Mr. Profitt alluded to it in his letter. That's the comparison of how Churchill is doing versus their competitors. Lots of numbers are used to compare competitors, for example, market shares, revenues, profits, return on investment. You would have to go to special sources to find these com-

parisons. It's realatively easy to get the size and trend information, at least, for the main numbers. The web site usually gives you that. The rest of the numbers require digging and calculations. That's beyond what I'm trying to help you learn."

"This all sounds like a lot of work."

"It can be. As I said before, you have to decide what's worth the effort.

One last thing about the numbers. They rarely give you answers or causes. They mostly point to symptoms. The power of numbers is, again, to give you good questions to ask."

"What if I don't even know the web site of the hospital?"

"Then, use a search engine like **www.google.com**. *That usually results in identifying the prospect's web site plus possibly other sites with useful information. You should probably do a general Internet search using the hospital's name even if you know the web site. This often results in useful articles about the hospital.*

You should also do an Internet search using the names of the executives you intend to visit. You might identify interesting tidbits about their backgrounds and their affiliations. This can help you prepare a better strategy to build rapport and even possibly give you an excellent way to get an appointment through a mutual connection."

"Whew, this is all a lot of information. I'm beginning to feel overwhelmed."

"Good point. I think it's time we stop and recap."

Any salesperson worth their salt will know my business.

CEO
Bank

REVIEW KEY POINTS

1. It is very risky to call on an executive with a blank page. Do some research into the hospital to show the executive you care enough to make the effort to better understand the business.

   You are trying to create the image that you are an expert in your business and how your business impacts the hospital's business. Ideally, you want to be viewed as a trusted advisor and as an agent of change for the executives and their staffs.

2. Sources of information:

   - Executives
   - Others in the organization
   - Outsiders who are in a position to know (suppliers, patients, competitors)
   - Hospital's own web site
   - Internet search

3. What to look for on the hospital's web site in the "About Us" or "Hospital Information" section:

   - Mission statement
   - Key executives and their résumés
   - Press releases and news
   - Statistical data like the number of beds and census
   - Financial highlights
   - CEO's letter

4. Print the CEO's letter; underline key items and make notes in the margins.

   - Key drivers
   - Goals and objectives

- Strategies
- Critical success factors (may have to be inferred)
- Other useful sales intelligence like executive changes, consolidations or expansion of locations, acquisitions and mergers

Look for the hospital's mission statement.

Look at the financial highlights; look for size, trends and comparisons.

Skim-read the descriptive section looking for useful sales intelligence.

All this information gives you indications as to where to spend time at the hospital and helps you to formulate interesting questions to ask people, especially executives.

5. Do a web search on the executive's name to possibly identify personal information and connections to use in building rapport and gaining access to the person.

6. Look for pains and gaps that you can relieve and fill in what the hospital is trying to do and how they are trying to get there.

DISCUSSION TOPICS

1. Pick several of your prospects, Go to each's web site. (Use **www.google.com** for a search if you don't know a web address.)

   Roam around each site to see what kind of information is available. Specifically look for the type of information listed in the Key Points 3.

2. For the hospitals you identified in Discussion Topic 1, do an Internet search to see what additional information you might find.

3. Select one important prospect. Go to that hospital's web site and print the CEO's letter. Analyze this letter for drivers, strategies, critical success factors and other useful sales intelligence.

   What is the date of the letter? If it is over three months old, access the press releases on the hospital's web site and print any commentary that updates the contents of the letter.

4. For the hospital analyzed in Discussion Topic 3, use the hospital's web site to identify their mission statement.

   Use the hospital's web site to identify trends in revenues and profits. What do these trends mean to your selling efforts?

5. Identify which executives you think you should meet. Access their résumés through the hospital's web site, and do a web search on their names to identify useful items about each executive and possible connections to use to gain access to the executives.

6. Based on your findings in Discussion Topics 3, 4, and 5, develop a set of questions for each targeted executive, building on what you have learned in your research.

CHAPTER 4:
WHO TO SEE AND WHEN

DO YOU REALLY NEED TO
CALL AT THE "C" LEVEL?

"**S**ely, you are sure making this executive call stuff look complex. I thought I wasn't supposed to be intimidated."

"No, Joe, you shouldn't be intimidated. Executives are people just like you. They have personal wants, needs and aspirations just like you do. What makes them different is that they have achieved status in their areas of expertise. That status gives them some power over what you want to do at their hospitals, namely, get them to buy your products and services. You have to give them good justifications so they'll exercise that power in your favor instead of against you.

Many salespeople are so intimidated by calling on executives that they avoid it like the plague. If that's the behavior of your competitors, then you have a wonderful opportunity to differentiate yourself at the executive level, both by what you sell and how you sell. Conversely, if your competitors are at the executive level, you definitely need to be there, too.

If the project is strategic to the company, than I would meet with a salesperson.

CEO
Computer Software Company

Don't forget: You are an expert in what you do. If their hospitals meet the qualifications for your products and services, then those executives should be talking with you, because you can help them personally achieve some part of their aspirations, and you can do some good for their businesses. Don't forget that salesman who was trying to sell a machine gun to that king. They really do need you."

"No, I won't forget that. If nothing else, you've instilled in me a sense of value and expertise so that I have a deeper belief in what I can do for people. I know I have to earn the right to an audience at the executive level. I think I'm ready to do that."

"Well, that brings up an interesting question. Do you really need to call at the executive level?"

"Now, wait a minute. It wasn't long ago that you said I wouldn't be risking much to call on executives in almost every sales opportunity. Are you going back on that?"

"Joe, I promised you when we began, that I would be realistic in everything we talk about. Realistically, it isn't necessary to call at the executive level in every or even most

opportunities. You may choose to do so because you want to be courteous or to establish a position just in case something goes wrong. But, necessary, no...desirable, probably yes.

There's an age-old sales axiom: Call high and broad. It should really say, Call as high and broad as you reasonably need to."

"I suspect you're getting at how much time and energy are necessary to win the business."

"Yes, that's the issue. I do suggest that you err on the conservative side and call higher and broader than might be needed. That's just good insurance. But calling on the executives just to do it isn't a good use of your time or theirs. You should have a good reason to go there."

"Give me some examples of good and bad reasons."

"OK. Here's a good one: If you really believe you have the right solution at the right price, and the lower level people aren't giving you a fair chance. Sound familiar? Churchill, maybe?

In this case, you need the power of an executive to keep the lower levels from making a mistake in choosing the wrong or an inferior solution."

"Wow. Talk about dangerous! I would be going over the heads of those lower level people. No matter how good I was at the executive level, they could kill me in some sneaky way."

"We'll talk about how to reduce the risk of an end-around strategy. But, for now, bear with me. I'm giving you examples of when it makes sense to go to an executive.

Here's another good situation for an executive call. If you suspect that a hospital has significant needs for your products and services, but they don't yet recognize those needs, then an executive call can be effective in opening a line of inquiry. This situation is an excellent way for you to demonstrate your expertise by suggesting new avenues for the executive to consider. That's like the salesman with the machine gun.

> **I would meet with Sales Representatives only if the project was indeed strategic to my organization, but strategic usually means a big initiative for us.**
>
> ***CEO***
> ***Hospital***

If you are in a significant competitive battle, making an effective call on an executive can create a personal preference for you and your offerings. The key word here is "effective." You better have something of value to present to the executive, and you better be able to clearly differentiate yourself, your company and your solutions from the competition.

There are times in relationships between your customers and your company when it makes sense for hospital executives to meet some of your management. It's part of building long-term relationships.

Another good time to call on an executive is immediately after you receive a significant order from the hospital, or when there's a big delivery, or when a major installation is completed. In all three cases, you are thanking them for the business and assuring them that you are staying on top of things to ensure they receive the value they expect.

Some really smart sales reps prepare an annual progress report for their more important accounts to present to the accounts' executives. In this report, the reps talk about the successes that have been achieved working together during the last year. They also point out any significant issues that might be current and what is being done to resolve them. The real kicker is the part of the presentation that talks about future opportunities to expand the relationship. The executives actually look forward to this kind of review."

"What about a situation where the budget isn't big enough to meet the need, or there's no budget to start with?"

I have reversed decisions on several occasions, not because of the lack of a good job by my people, but sometimes, negotiations break down, and I need another place to go. It helps if I have a relationship with the salesperson on that team.

Vice President, Marketing
Airline

"Yes, an executive visit could certainly clear the air in those kinds of situations. You better have a good cost justification strategy in both of those cases."

"Sometimes, lower level people initiate an investigation without the knowledge of their boss, hoping that they can build a case to get the boss to approve the procurement. A call to the executive can quickly establish if this is a pipe dream or if the executive is open-minded if the project can be justified."

"It sounds like I should go to an executive every time. Is there any time I *wouldn't* go?"

"There's no need to go to the top when the deal is a low-level, tactical purchase with little strategic interest. In these situations, the executives usually delegate the decision and the budget to lower level people to execute. Sometimes, the purchasing department handles the whole thing in these cases. The executive doesn't want to hear about it again. He or she assumes everything is okay and the need will be fulfilled."

"Well, what if it isn't okay? Would I elevate it then?"

"You could, if you are elevating the situation because a serious error was about to be made at the lower level. Again, you better have your facts clear and your justification strong for bringing to the executive what he or she thought was no problem. Executives don't like these kind of pop-up problems.

Another situation not requiring an executive visit is when you have the deal in the bag. Of course, you can choose to call on an executive as insurance. That's your decision to make, presumably in concert with the lower level people who are supporting you."

"What I'm getting out of all this is that I should normally include an executive visit in my sales strategy unless there's a good reason not to."

"That's a good way of putting it, Joe."

WHO TO VISIT

"That also brings up two big questions: which executives should you visit, and when should you do so?"

"Who do you think you should visit at Churchill?"

"Well, it's pretty obvious that I need to visit Ms. Heather Hanks, the new VP of Operations. It's her department that will be buying the new equipment. All the selection committee members report to her somewhere in her organizational chain. Besides, that's probably where that bum from Super Solutions has been spending his time."

"Yes, clearly the executive who has the most to gain from your products and services should be on your call list.

It might be a good idea to have a better understanding of Churchill's organization than that the committee members report to Ms. Hanks "somewhere in the chain." If you are going to set a winning strategy, you should have an understanding of who reports to whom and who has what power."

"Yeah, yeah. I'll get all that from my friend on the committee."

"Good idea. You might want to cross-check what your friend tells you so that you are acting on good input.

Any other executive important to you at Churchill?"

"I should probably see the guy with the money, the CFO. And, while I'm at it, a call on the CEO might be a good way to trump that Super Solutions guy."

"This is probably a good time to clear up any confusion you might have regarding the Chief Executive Officer and the Chief Financial Officer."

"Who says I'm confused?"

"Let's just make sure we're talking about the same thing.

Let's start with the financial officer. The financial executive might be called the Vice President of Finance or the CFO or some similar title. He or she has a couple of responsibilities that might be important to you.

First, this executive is the person responsible for managing the hospital's cash flow. It's important to understand that the CFO does not own any budgets except the one for his or her own department. The other budgets are owned by the responsible executives. But, the CFO is responsible for making sure that there is cash to fund all the budgets.

So, in the case of Churchill, it's probably Ms. Hanks, the VP of Operations, who owns the budget that would be used to buy your MegaDoppel, not the CFO.

It still might be useful to call on the CFO, especially if you have some particular financing plan to help a hospital to more easily acquire your products and services. The CFO will be the person who ultimately approves using that financing plan.

Another important role for the CFO is that of an internal auditor of all the departments in the hospital. In this role, the CFO makes sure that all the executives and their operations wisely use the hospital's assets. If the CFO see problems, he or she tries to work it out with the appropriate executive, or, if that doesn't work, then the CFO raises the issue to the CEO for resolution. The CFO is usually a close confidante with the CEO, so the CFO generally has a lot of power in the organization.

So, you might want to visit the CFO to present how your solution can improve life at the hospital. This is also the place to present a good cost justification to show the CFO the wisdom of agreeing with your solution.

Again, be aware that the CFO usually doesn't own the budget that will pay for your products and services, unless it's the CFO's own department that will be using them."

"Oh, yeah? Have you ever dealt with a purchasing department? They act like they own the budget and the decision."

"True, a purchasing department makes sure the terms and conditions are acceptable, and they process the paperwork. In this role, they might give you a hard time and drive a tough bargain. They'll give you the impression that they're running the whole procurement and that it's their decision. As I said before, with non-strategic procurements, it often is their decision. But, with strategic procurements, it's the operational department that normally owns the budget and decides what to buy, as long as the cost is within the approved budget. Purchasing may still have a voice in the decision, so you have to work with them and give them a win.

> **I only see sales reps who I think can impact the future of my business. Anything that is tactical to my business, I usually send to a subordinate.**
>
> *CEO*
> *Financial Institution*

Now, the CFO can raise questions about a particular purchase planned by the operating department. And, the CFO can definitely wave a big red flag if there's not enough budget to pay for the desired products and services or if the CFO doesn't believe the purchase is cost justified.

In summary, the CFO makes sure your products and services fit within the authorized budget, and he or she will be the right person to deal with for any special way to pay for those products and services. And, of course, the purchasing people will give you grief to get the best pricing and the best terms and conditions. But, don't lose sight of the fact that the operational executive usually owns the budget and makes the ultimate decision on what products and services are needed to fulfill that executive's responsibilities.

Is that clear, Joe?"

"Yes, I think so. What you're telling me is that, for things like the MegaDoppel, the CFO is not the usual decision maker. The CFO can be a friend or enemy depending on how the CFO sees the user department justifying the MegaDoppel. The CFO can also be a friend if I can present a useful way to conserve the hospital's cash, like an attractive leasing plan, which I happen to have for the MegaDoppel. So, it looks like the CFO is one of those executives I should visit.

Do I have it right?"

"Right on target.

Now, let's look at the Chief Executive Officer or CEO. For your purposes, the CEO is the ultimate strategist for the hospital. He or she is the visionary...the cheerleader...the coach who rallies the employees to achieve the goals and objectives of the hospital.

Normally, you wouldn't meet the CEO unless you had something very important to the CEO's personal interests, like a pet project or a very important strategy that the CEO was closely tracking. You would normally call on the other executives whose responsibilities were closer to what your products and services impact.

This caution is not to suggest avoiding the CEO. It's just to suggest that you should carefully consider whether or not a visit to the CEO will really help you.

Also, be aware that sometimes the role of the CEO is split with a Chief Operations Officer, or COO. The COO usually takes responsibility for the short-term success of the business. The CEO, in this case, really is a futurist and goodwill ambassador to the external world.

Now, the COO could be someone who you might seriously consider visiting because of his or her operational responsibilities."

"Well, I guess it really depends on how much of an impact I am going to have on their business as to whom I should think about meeting. I guess it also depends on the size of the hospital. I doubt I would ever meet the CEO of Mayo Clinic. But I might meet Mr. Profitt, the CEO of Churchill."

"You are definitely getting the idea.

Anyone else you might visit at Churchill?"

"I already have the VP of Operations, the CFO, maybe the CEO. Don't you think that's enough?"

"It doesn't matter what I think. It's what time and energy you think you need to invest in developing and securing a particular piece of business.

I'm not suggesting you do so, but in Mr. Profitt's letter, it seems that the business development people have a big stake in how effective and efficient the operations are and how well the services are delivered. While the VP of Business Development is not the decision maker for your MegaDoppel, he or she could provide valuable insight into cost justifications for it. This executive might also put a good word in for you. But, you have to decide if it's worth the time and effort.

The point of all this is that "the who" to visit in the executive suite is a sales strategy question for you to decide. The easy ones are those who own the budget and manage the operations where your product and services will have impact. Others could be useful in giving you intelligence or support. In each case, just make sure you have a good reason for them to meet with you. They have to get value out of your visit, or you're just wasting their time."

"I understand. Well, now that we've finished, I better get back to my sales strategy planning. I have some important calls to make if I'm going to turn around this disaster at Churchill. Thanks for all the help. Bye, Sely."

"Uh, Joe, I certainly applaud your enthusiasm and your eagerness to act, but there are a couple of other things to review before you go charging off."

"Like what?"

"Well, there's that little question of when should you visit an executive."

TIMING IS IMPORTANT

"That's a no-brainer for me. I've got to get there now! This deal is going down a rathole for me."

"Yes, when you are in serious trouble, a call to an executive might provide you with new hope and direction. But, let's take it out of the context of Churchill. Hopefully, not all your sales opportunities will be dire emergencies.

In general, when is it a good time to call on an executive?"

"In my sales class, the instructor said I should always start high in the organization, because that gives me more power with the lower level people."

"As with all sales strategy considerations, the questions are what are the risks and what are the benefits of calling high to start a sales cycle at a prospect? How can you minimize the risks and maximize the benefits?"

"The benefit is obvious, assuming I make a good call. I'll probably be asked to talk with someone else in the exec's organization. The exec might even arrange the appointment. Whether the exec does that or not, I'll be talking to the lower level person at the invitation of that person's boss. That's real power. It definitely will get me attention."

"And the risk?"

"Well, if I make a bad call at the executive level, I'm probably in big trouble for that opportunity."

"Yes, you certainly wouldn't have the executive's endorsement at lower levels, and you will have a hard time meeting that executive again.

How do you maximize the benefits and minimize the risks?"

"It's doing what we've been talking about all this time. Doing my homework. Not walking in with a blank page. Talking about how I can help the exec achieve something important to him or her. That maximizes the benefits and minimizes the risks."

"Joe, I can see light at the end of the tunnel. You are definitely getting the messages.

I like to meet suppliers at the beginning of the buying cycle, because it helps me understand what are the available solutions to my problems. I usually don't meet with that many during the selection process, but I always meet with the finalist.

CEO
Financial Institution

In general, executives tend to be more involved with a project in the beginning than in the middle. They want to have a better understanding of the business issues and a high-level understanding of the alternatives to solving those issues. They also want to be involved in setting the criteria of how a solution will be decided.

Once the executives have exerted this level of involvement, they usually delegate the detailed investigation to their subordinates. Other than an occasional progress report, they aren't usually involved in the hot and heavy competitive battle that you fight, unless problems arise.

They don't like it when problems arise, because they would rather be dealing with more pleasant things than working on problems that they didn't expect. What they do expect is that their subordinates will implement the defined strategy without any further executive involvement other than occasional reviews.

So, the message for you, Joe, is that you'll have a better chance of an executive audience early in the con-

sideration of a hospital's needs than after the search for a solution has been delegated down. Now, this doesn't mean you can't get to an executive in the middle of the selection process. It just means that it's more difficult to secure the appointment, because it implies that the lower level people are having problems doing the selection job.

That's also why the lower level folks might try to block you from seeing their boss. They've been given the job to do the search and selection. You going above them makes it look like they aren't doing their job. That's a big threat.

Your reasons for getting the appointment in the middle of the sales cycle need to be very compelling. Your risks are also higher, both in terms of offending and alienating the lower level people and in terms of being the messenger of bad news or a problem to the executive. In this case, they may shoot the messenger!"

The salespeople whom I do see could be at the beginning or at the end. Often, I agree to a visit after all the selection is done. It is my job to further investigate what kind of partner they will be for my company. In some cases, I have completely changed the decision of the selection committee based on that investigation and gone with a completely different supplier.

CEO
Computer Software Company

"It sounds like I should start at the top early in the game or forget calling high."

"Be careful with generalizations. Every sales situation is unique. Just recognize the benefits and risks and be smart in how you maximize the benefits and minimize the risks in each situation.

96

Go into every visit with one or two suggested next steps. Be proactive. Show the executive you are an advisor with actions in mind.

Don't stuff your ideas down the executive's throat. Give the executive your ideas as possible alternatives and seek his or her concurrence or other reactions.

Start at the top when you have a compelling story to begin your efforts. Maybe it's something you read in the CEO's letter that triggers your interest, or maybe it's something told to you by another hospital. Or, it might be a success at a similar hospital that you think could also fit this prospect.

Any time there's a new executive in an area important to you, think strongly about visiting him or her. That's when they will be particularly open to new ideas.

If you're not sure where to go in a hospital or what to emphasize, then the safer route is to start lower in the organization to learn more before you tackle the top.

But, remember, this is not a black and white issue. Do what you believe will advance your cause and will create the best value for your prospect."

"One of the reasons the sales class instructor said to start high is that I would avoid the problem of going around lower level people who would be threatened by me calling higher. If I start at the top, there's no going around. I'm already there.

"How do I handle that problem if I don't start at the top?"

"First, you should have the right attitude and establish early in your dealings with the lower levels the expectation that you'll be visiting the executives. Act and talk like a business advisor who is confident and accustomed to working with executives.

Don't say something like, 'I'll be visiting your executives to get first-hand what they think.'

Rather, try something like, 'Let's work together to better define what is needed and what is a solid, justified solution so that, when we visit your executives, they are confident we are on the right track.'

You are putting the lower level person on notice that you intend to visit the executives. But, you're not shutting him or her out. The person is part of the action with a solid business recommendation to make to the boss. You actually want the person to sponsor your visit to the executive. The person has the opportunity to look smart by bringing you and your solutions to the attention of the boss."

"What if that person asks why I need to go to the executive or says that an executive visit isn't necessary?"

"You might say, 'In my experience with something as important as this project, it is a definite benefit to you and the project if your executive has the opportunity to meet a potential supplier in person. That shows him (or her) the caliber of people you are considering. It also gives him (or her) the opportunity to directly ask any questions.'

See, you're representing the visit as a benefit to the lower level person.

Of course, the person might still be gun-shy of you visiting the boss. If you show the individual that you are capable and earn the person's trust, then that concern usually goes away.

But, there might be situations where the lower level people don't want you to go to the higher level, period.

I typically meet with sales reps in the beginning of a strategic initiative to see what the playing field looks like. Then, as the finalists start to form, I will meet with reps from those companies.

Vice President, Marketing
Airline

I tend to meet with sales reps when the field has been narrowed down.

CEO
Hospital

It might simply be that the boss told the lower level people that he or she didn't want to see salespeople. The subordinates have been totally tasked with the job.

Or, worse, maybe the project really hasn't been approved by the boss, in which case you may be wasting time on a pipe dream. Or, maybe your competitor is the preferred solution, in which case the lower level folks don't want you messing up the situation with their boss."

"I think that last possibility is my situation at Churchill. The committee wants Super Solutions and they don't want me throwing a monkey wrench in the deal. Now what do I do?"

"First, you have to weigh the risks of going around the committee versus the benefits to be achieved by such a visit.

If they haven't told you not to, then you can just do it and plead ignorance of their wishes.

If they have actually told you not to call higher, then you can use an age-old selling technique of bringing your manager to the meeting and pleading that he made you do it. While that strategy isn't totally clean, it does reduce the blame on you.

In the Churchill situation, there doesn't appear to be much risk. If you don't do something dramatic and decisive, you'll lose the business anyway.

But, you should be prepared for a possible hostile situation. Some of the committee members might be at the meeting. Remember, the boss thought the situation was under control and that there were no problems. You showing up, with or without your manager, implies a problem exists that caused the need for the meeting.

It may turn out to be a very pleasant and positive meeting. Hope for the best and be prepared for the worst."

I typically will meet with salespeople in the beginning of a project to get the lay of the land, but I will let my people do the selection from the RFP's and presentations. Sometimes, I will sit in on a few of those presentations. I almost always meet with the finalists for a personality fit: who I trust the most and think will be a good partner.

CIO
Retailer

"Right. I'm going to call Ms. Hanks, the VP of Operations, right now. They need me. I have a better solution than Super Solutions. It may cost a little more, but Churchill will get much more of what they need with the MegaDoppel. It's dumb for them to buy anything else. Where's the phone? I'm calling her."

"Joe, I think you can wait another minute or two. There are a few more tidbits to help make that call more effective."

"By the time we finish with all your little tidbits, Super Solutions will be installing their junk! Now what?"

"Oh, just the little matter of what are you going to say if Ms. Hanks picks up the telephone when it rings? Or, what will you say if her administrative assistant picks up the telephone?"

"I guess you don't want to hear that I'll just wing it. (Sigh) Okay. What do you want me to do?"

"It's time to talk about how to get the appointment with an executive and how to open the dialogue in case the exec does pick up the phone.

But, first, let's recap where we are."

REVIEW KEY POINTS

1. Good reasons to call at the executive level:

    To bring to the executive a new opportunity with strategic value to the executive and the hospital which deserves developing

    To create competitive differentiation

    To get a budget established or to increase an inadequate budget by presenting a compelling business case

    To qualify that a need really exists and that there is intent to fulfill the need

    To prevent the lower levels from making a bad or sub-optimal choice

    To build relationships

    To thank the executive for the business and to assure the executive you are on top of things

    To present an annual progress report, reviewing the past year's achievements and identifying new opportunities for the future

2. Consider visiting the following executives:

    Any executive who owns the budget and whose operation is directly impacted by your solution

    Chief Financial Officer (CFO) if you have a special financing option or if you need to help the operational department cost-justify your solution

Chief Executive Officer (CEO) and Chief Operations Officer (COO) if the project is very strategic to the hospital or if it is a pet project of the CEO or COO

Executives who can provide you with important intelligence or support because their operations are impacted by your solution, even though not as heavily nor as directly

3. The most likely time to get the executive appointment is early in the need consideration, especially before a formal search for a solution has started. At this early time, the executives are interested in better understanding the need and what possible alternatives exist to fulfill the need. They are also interested in defining criteria to decide what is the best solution.

    To get an executive appointment later in the sales cycle requires a more compelling reason, because the executive assumes the lower level people are doing their jobs in the search and evaluation of possible solutions. An executive visit at this time inherently implies that there is a problem in the process.

4. How to execute an "end-around" visit when a lower level person is blocking you:

    Try not to get into the situation in the first place by establishing early in the sales cycle that you expect to visit the executives; earn trust and confidence with the lower level people that you can make an effective visit to their bosses.

Decide whether the executive visit really is important to your strategy. If you are losing anyway, then what more harm can such a visit cause?

If you have not been explicitly told not to, then go do it and plead ignorance that there was a problem with you making such a visit.

If explicitly forbidden to make an executive visit, then have your manager make the appointment and accompany him or her on the call; you can blame your manager for the deed if the lower level people protest.

Be prepared for a hostile environment. Lower level people might be in attendance.

5. Timing of an executive call is important. You usually don't have a *carte blanche* to call as often as you want, so carefully consider your shots.

   It is generally a good strategy to start at the top if you are well-equipped with information and you suspect there is a strong strategic need for your solutions.

   It is a good strategy to start at the top if the hospital is not aware of a potentially important opportunity that you want to bring to an executive's attention to begin an inquiry.

   It is generally better to start at a lower level if your information is scant. But, you should plan on calling higher as soon as you have enough information to make an effective call.

DISCUSSION TOPICS

1. Select one of your important prospect opportunities, possibly the one you analyzed at the end of
   Chapter 3. If you have not already done so, select
   which executives you want to visit. Define what
   value you anticipate getting out of each visit and
   what value each executive will get from talking with
   you. Are both values compelling? Do you think each
   executive would agree with your assessment of
   those values?

2. For the prospect opportunity in Discussion Topic 1,
   what will you say to any lower level people who
   might question your efforts to visit their bosses? If
   you were in their shoes, would you be convinced
   by your statements?

3. Select one of your prospect opportunities that is
   very early in the sales cycle or possibly not even
   started. Which executives do you want to visit now?
   What compelling reasons to you have to get them
   to agree to such visits?

CHAPTER 5:
GETTING THE APPOINTMENT

WHY IS IT SO HARD TO GET
AN EXECUTIVE APPOINTMENT?

"Joe, salespeople often wonder why it's so hard to get an executive call appointment."

"It's hard? Just pick up the phone and get the appointment. What's the big deal?"

I meet with existing strategic suppliers on a regular basis because, often, they have solutions that can be helpful to my organization or our future direction. I try to have a consolidated supplier group that I can rely on. I always go to them first with new initiatives. They are also helpful in advising me on how to solve problems.

CEO
Hospital

"Well, to continue being honest and realistic with you, it is a big deal. It goes back to what we started with: drivers, strategies and critical success factors.

Executives are very busy people with those drivers, strategies and CSFs. On top of that, they have internal political battles to wage. They have many constituencies demanding their attention and time.

They often have to exercise triage on the things making those demands. When you pop up on their radar screen asking for their time, it's very easy to put you far down, even off, the priority list. There are just too many other known items demanding immediate attention to add an unknown, you.

To protect their time, they hire very efficient administrative assistants who are experts at screening attempts to reach their bosses to take away valuable time. It's not just outsiders like you who are screened. Even internal people, including subordinates, must show good cause to get on the executive's meeting calendar.

That's why it's so hard for a sales rep to get an appointment. The assumption is automatic: this salesperson is trying to get an appointment to bias the executive and the hospital to the salesperson's own product and services. It's a one-way meeting just to the salesperson's benefit. Therefore, it's a waste of the executive's time. Kill it."

"I don't think that's what's going to happen when I try to meet Ms. Hanks. I have some very important information that she needs to know. Otherwise, Churchill will be making a big mistake."

"You may know that, Joe, but no one else at Churchill does...or, at least, no one important has yet agreed

with that claim. Your task is to make a compelling case with Ms. Hanks or with her screener so that you do get the appointment. And, you'll have only about 30 seconds to do it."

"You're scaring me. A few moments ago, you had me convinced I should be calling on executives. Now, you're telling me getting the appointment is harder than scaling Mt. Everest. Just what are you talking about?"

"It comes down to how to get the executive's attention and willingness to spend time with you. Two pieces go into that puzzle: the who and the what."

THE "WHO" AND THE "WHAT" OF GETTING AN EXECUTIVE APPOINTMENT

"The 'who' and the 'what'? C'mon. This isn't the time for guessing games. I've got an order to save!"

If it is a project where it is obvious that we have to go outside of our normal suppliers, I will typically agree to meet the salespeople if they are persistent enough. It is hard enough keeping relationships with my existing suppliers, so, they have to be a potential partner before I would agree to it.

Chief Procurement Officer
Defense Contractor

"A little patience, Joe, and the path will become crystal clear.

The 'who' refers to who helps you to get the appointment. The 'what' refers to the compelling message that you must deliver.

Let's start with the 'who.' You are much more likely to get an appointment if someone the executive knows and respects introduces you.

Unfortunately, cold calls, even those preceded by a letter or email, aren't very effective in getting an appointment. They are most likely screened out by the administrative assistant. But, if you have no other choice, that's what you have to try, using a very compelling opening statement.

Better than a cold call is an introduction. Someone from the executive's own hospital is the most likely to work. This could be a subordinate or a person from a different part of the hospital. Either way, it's the most likely way to get the appointment, but by no means a guarantee.

Salespeople who leave long-winded messages are wasting their time. The good ones are succinct on why they are calling me and lay it out as to why I should give them my time. They have a compelling, specific reason why they need to meet them. I respect that.

CIO
Retailer

An introduction from someone outside the executive's hospital is useful, especially if it's a peer or someone the executive respects. That's one of the reasons you should try to find a biography of the executive you want to meet so that you might identify connections like college chums or mutual charitable or service group memberships.

Given the old adage that 'kings like to talk to kings,' you have a better chance of getting a meeting if an executive in your organization made the cold contact to the target executive. Of course, your executives expect you to be making those contacts, not them, so you'll need a very compelling reason for your own executive to make the effort.

And, if your company is already a supplier to the executive's organization, that increases your chances of getting the appointment, especially if you've done good things at the hospital."

"That's certainly a bleak picture. Cold calls are losers. And, unless I have a good friend, highly placed and well-respected in the hospital, I'm probably not going to get an appointment."

"That's not what I said. I said that the probabilities significantly improve over a cold call if you are already known at the hospital from previous successful business or if someone can recommend you, especially if it's an insider at the hospital.

Cold calls can work. Just ask for the meeting and you might get it. If you don't ask for it, I'm pretty sure you won't get it. You'd be surprised at how many salespeople just don't ask for the meeting because they assume they won't get it or they are afraid of rejection.

A lot of sales reps like to send a letter or email first, because it gives them something to reference in the follow up try for the appointment. In a little while, I'll show you what such a letter might look like.

If you choose to send a letter to introduce yourself and your compelling reason for a visit, you might include a germane article or literature that would help the executive to appreciate the importance of what you're offering. But, if you do send printed material, highlight the key points you want the executive to see. Don't expect the executive to plow through the whole thing looking for the nuggets.

By the way, sending highlighted articles and literature is a good technique to keep in touch with an executive as long as you don't overload him or her with paper. You could do it through email, as well, but then, just send the important excerpts, not the whole thing. They appreciate useful information. But, remember, they already have tons of things to read and absorb. Be very selective in what you send."

"One trick that a guy in our office uses is to call an executive either before or after the hospital's normal business hours. He sometimes even tries on weekends, because execs often are there then. What do you think of that?"

"Well, you have a good chance of avoiding the administrative assistant screen and having the executive answer his or her own telephone. But, you better be ready with your compelling statement, because you will have about 30 seconds before you lose the executive's attention.

Another idea I've seen work is to arrange your timing so that you and the executive get into the elevator together at his or her office building. You need a good 'elevator pitch' for this to work."

"Elevator pitch? Give me an example."

OK, let's assume it's Ms. Hanks whom you just happen to encounter in the elevator. You might say something like, 'Good morning, Ms. Hanks, I'm Joe Repp with Mega Systems. I've been working with your team on the workflow upgrade project. I was going to ask your administrative assistant to arrange a little time for us to meet to discuss some critical aspects of this project. When would be a good time for us to spend a few minutes?'

Now, she might ask you to call her administrative assistant to set a time or to check her availability. Or, she might just invite you right then. She could also ask a question like, 'What do you mean by critical aspects?'

It is rare that I meet with any sales rep unless they are recommended by my contemporaries or by my directors. My staff screens everything for me. I never answer a call on my own. I do read emails and listen to voice mails daily, but they are pre-screened, so if someone wants to get to me, they have to get past my staff.

CEO
Hospital

And, that brings us to the 'what' of our little appointment puzzle, because however you make the contact, what you say next is crucial."

"The 'who' was bad enough."

"If you've done your homework, Joe, the 'what' is a lot easier.

The more you know about the personal needs and aspirations of the executive and the more you can directly connect your products and services as enablers of those needs, then you have a powerful attention-getting opening that increases the probability of getting the appointment. It's back to those drivers, strategies and critical success factors."

"Give me some examples of what you mean."

"I'd rather you gave me the examples, but I'll get your thinking started. Remember, you're the expert, the advisor, in what you do and how it impacts your customer.

Let's assume I make a cold call and Ms. Hanks at Churchill picks up the telephone.

Here's what is not a good idea to say: 'Ms. Hanks, I am calling you to tell you how I can make you successful. Your operation needs to be more efficient and needs to improve the quality of its processes. I can make those things happen. I can meet with you this week or next. Which is better for you?' That's a very risky statement. It makes you more than confident. It makes you look cocky and presumptuous.

You want to be confident; you want to show you've done some homework; and, you want to show your consultative ability.

A better opening might be, 'Ms. Hanks, I am calling to bring to your attention a way to help make your operation more efficient with higher quality. I and my company have been able to assist XYZ Hospital to achieve just those results with a payback in less than 12 months. From what I've read in Mr. Profitt's latest letter on Churchill's web site, lower cost to produce and improved quality can be major factors in increasing Churchill's competitive position in the marketplace. I would like to spend 30 minutes with

Salespeople get to me two ways: one way is they sell my assistant on the reasons they need to see me; two, they are recommended by an associate of mine. The meeting is always scheduled [executive assistant]. I know most executives let their assistants screen calls, but I usually listen to all the voice mails from salespeople and either forward them to the appropriate parties to take care of, if I think it is interesting to the enterprise, or tell Barbara to set a meeting, or to call them to tell them we are not interested.

CEO
Computer Software Company

you to explore this opportunity in more detail. Would this week or next be more convenient for you?'

Notice that I picked up on Ms. Hank's personal hot buttons of production efficiency and improved quality. If she can do that, she's a heroine at Churchill. I gave her a meaningful reference with an indication of how a solution can be cost-justified: the payback. And, I gave Ms. Hanks the benefit of being more competitive, so that she can view this opportunity as good corporate citizenship."

"Oh, you smooth tongue!"

"Actually, the likelihood of getting the appointment based on this statement alone is very low. What I'm hoping is that she will ask me a question to begin qualifying what I've claimed. When she starts doing that, then I have a much higher probability of an appointment, assuming I answer her questions satisfactorily; or, at least, I hope to pique her interest enough that she'll send me to meet one of her subordinates, usually one level below her.

If she sends me to one of her subordinates, then I'll end with something like, 'After I meet with Mr. Jones, I will report back to you.' That way, I keep the possibility of an appointment open. Even if she says something about Jones telling her what transpires, I've still left the door open."

"But what if she answers your opening by saying she isn't interested?"

"I might say something like, 'Ms. Hanks, I realize you are a very busy executive with high priorities that need your immediate attention. Rather than totally miss these opportunities for efficiency and quality, with whom on your staff might I start to explore the possibilities? That way, your time is conserved and your staff can qualify my claims and XYZ's results.'

At this point, she might hang up on me, or she might ask me to send her something in the mail, which is often a delaying tactic and an attempt to get me back into the screening process. If she hangs up on me, I'll still send her information and then try again, working through the screen by confirming the material was received and referencing my earlier call to Ms. Hanks. The same strategy is appropriate if she asks me to send her something, only I'll specifically reference Ms. Hanks' request for the information when I talk with her assistant.

You have to be a persistent bulldog, Joe. You have to steel yourself against rejection and press on with what you believe in. Of course, you also have to be careful not to make yourself an unbearable pest. Be professional and friendly."

"Hmm. What if you call and you get the horrible administrative assistant?"

"First, Joe, get out of your head the notion that the administrative assistant is your enemy. This person can be a very important and useful resource to you. You have to sell the person on your value. Treat the administrative assistant as if you were directly talking with the executive. It's smart sales strategy to build a rela-

tionship with this person, even before you're ready to call on the executive. The assistant is often a powerful doorkeeper who can open those doors as well as keep them closed.

If my assistant is not impressed, then I never see the salesperson.

CEO
Financial Institution

I meet more often with those salespeople who are recommended by someone that I know. I very rarely schedule a meeting myself. I do, however, direct my assistant from time to time as to which meetings that I want to schedule.

Vice President, Operations
Financial Investment
Company

So, Joe, tell me, how would you start if Ms. Hanks' admin assistant picks up the telephone? I'll play the role of Ms. Smith, the assistant."

"Actually, her name is Kathy. Well, let's see. I'm going to build on that nice statement you had. Here goes.

Kathy, my name is Joe Repp and I represent Mega Systems Corporation. I'm calling to speak with Ms. Hanks."

"Does Ms. Hanks know you, Mr. Repp?"

"We haven't met, but I have a very important opportunity to discuss with her that will significantly improve her operations."

"Well, Mr. Repp, Ms. Hanks is unavailable right now. Why don't you send her some information in the mail?"

"That's not what I want. OK, smart guy, let's see if you do it. This time, I'll be the assistant."

"Good morning, Kathy. My name is Sely Sharpe and I represent Mega Systems Corporation. Kathy, I know that Ms. Hanks is a very busy executive. I am calling to bring to her attention a way to help make her operations more efficient with higher quality results. I and my company have been able to assist XYZ Hospital to achieve just those results with a payback in less than 12 months. From what I've read in Mr. Profitt's letter on Churchill's web site, lower cost and improved quality can be major factors in increasing Churchill's competitive position in the marketplace. I'd like to spend 30 minutes with Ms. Hanks to explore this opportunity in more detail. How do you suggest I go about arranging such an appointment?"

"Heh, heh. Watch this!

Does Ms. Hanks know you, Mr. Sharpe?"

My assistant handles all of my telephone and letter correspondence. I have, on occasion, taken calls from salespeople, but they always go through my assistant first. If they want to get to me, they have to get by her first. Email is another story. I at least glance at sales requests on email. I have returned a few that ended up doing business with us, but most of the time I refer them on.

CEO
Bank

"No, Kathy, we have never had the pleasure of meeting. But, it is an opportunity of significant value to her and to Churchill that we do have that pleasure. What do you suggest?"

"Why don't you send her some information in the mail?"

"I can certainly do that. In fact, because this opportunity is very time sensitive, I will email (or fax) it within the next hour. Would you be so kind as to let her know

that I called and bring the email to her attention. Then, I will telephone you later today to see what she prefers. I really appreciate your assistance in bringing this opportunity to her attention. It is definitely not a waste of time."

"Hmmph. So, what have you achieved that I didn't? You were screened out, too."

"Well, not quite the same. I still have the possibility of meeting Ms. Hanks. The administrative assistant will be hard pressed not to show Ms. Hanks the information that I'm sending. And, I have the opportunity to call back later in the day.

Now, when I do call back, I'll confirm that Ms. Hanks has seen the material. If not, I'll schedule another callback, again nicely asking Kathy to bring the information to Ms. Hanks' attention.

If Kathy tells me that Ms. Hanks has seen the material but doesn't have time for an appointment, I'll ask Kathy who would be the most appropriate person on Ms. Hanks' staff to see to do some qualification of my claims and the results at XYZ. Then, when I speak with that person, I'll say that I've been asked to speak with him or her by Ms. Hanks' office. That will add some weight for me to get the appointment with the subordinate.

If Kathy says that Ms. Hanks is not interested in what I have to offer, then I am out of the ball game as far as meeting Ms. Hanks at this time. If I really do believe that I have something important for Churchill, I can still go to the lower levels to begin my sales efforts there.

Remember, all these examples have assumed a totally cold call. If you have some positive experience in Churchill to reference, then it makes the request for an appointment more persuasive. And, of course, if you have someone to recommend you or introduce you, then your chances for an appointment increase dramatically. But, regardless, you need compelling reasons and solid references, which gets back to doing your homework."

A COMPELLING INTRODUCTORY LETTER/EMAIL

"Earlier you mentioned a sample, introductory letter or email. What would that look like?"

"It essentially builds on the same thing as the compelling statement you would make on the telephone. Here's an example."

"Note several things in this letter. First, the focus of the letter starts on Ms. Hanks and Churchill. The word 'I' doesn't appear until much later in the letter. Second, the points I picked to stress should be hot buttons for Ms. Hanks. My research into Churchill should help ensure that, but what executive would say that lowering cost and improving quality are unimportant?

Third, I used a reference, XYZ Hospital. As much as possible, this reference should be impressive to Ms. Hanks in terms of the prestige of XYZ in the industry and how similar XYZ's processes are to those of Churchill. Of course, you would get XYZ's permission before you used them as a reference.

MEGA SYSTEMS

Dear Ms. Hanks:

Based on Mr. Profitt's comments in his latest letter on Churchill's web site, your operations appear to be a central element of the Hospital's strategy to increase market share across all of your markets. It seems that workflow efficiency and process quality are critical to the hospital's success.

Our company, Mega Systems, has a long and successful history of working with hospitals like Churchill to achieve just those types of results. Recently, we assisted XYZ Hospital to lower the their process costs and to increase process quality. These efforts resulted in a payback of less than 12 months!

I would like to spend 30 minutes with you to explore specifically what we have in mind that could enhance your workflow to lower costs and to increase quality.

Enclosed is brief background on Mega Systems. I have underlined the particularly pertinent points.

I will call your office early next week to arrange an appointment. You can reach me at (telephone number.)

I look forward to meeting you to explore how we can work together to enable Churchill to be much more competitive in the marketplace.

Very truly yours,

Joe Repp

I included some literature, which I highlighted. And I am taking the action to contact her, although I've given her the information if she wants to contact me first.

This is a useful format for a cold-contact executive letter or email. Now, when I call for the appointment, I can reference the letter, whether I talk directly with Ms. Hanks or with her administrative assistant."

"One thing I like about the letter approach is that it gives me something tangible to reference."

"Yes, Joe, that's a value. But, you shouldn't assume the executive ever saw the letter. When you telephone, you still need to use your compelling statement, only it starts with the phrase, 'As I suggested in my letter to you...' "

"OK, Sely, I see that it's not a pushover to get the appointment, especially if it's really a cold call. Still, I think I'm ready to take on Ms. Hanks and Churchill. I'll get my friend on the committee to recommend me to her.

I never pay attention to letters unless I have been looking to get more information anyway from the type of supplier.

CEO
Computer Software Company

I don't think that I have ever responded to a hard copy letter. I have, however, responded to emails, usually telling one of my subordinates that they should have a look.

Vice President, Operations
Financial Investment
Company

I always read my own mail and email. I never answer my office phone and always answer my cell phone.

CEO
Financial Institution

And I'll treat Kathy, her administrative assistant, with great respect. See you later."

I very seldom read letters anymore. Email is almost in that same category, because I get so many of them. If they do send me an email, it had better grab my attention in the first sentence. The best ones are name-dropping someone that is relevant to me, like so-and-so suggested that I write you about this important business problem that I can solve.

Chief Procurement Officer
Defense Contractor

I do not respond to letters. I get hundreds of them, and most are marketing literature. If it is a piece that has a solution that we are already looking for, then I might pass on to others. Email has become the same.

CIO
Retailer

"Uh, Joe, I agree you are almost ready, but there is just a little more that can make the difference for you to be successful at the executive levels.

First, let me just summarize what we've discussed in this chapter."

"Chapter?"

"Yes, Joe, life is a book. We have just added another chapter."

REVIEW KEY POINTS

1. In descending order of preference, here are ways to get to an executive:

   Internal introduction or reference
   External introduction or reference from a peer or respected mutual contact
   Call from one of your executives to the hospital executive
   Letter or email from you or one of your executives followed by your telephone call
   Cold call

2. If you use a cold call, try to call when the administrative assistant is not there to screen your call.

3. If you do speak to the administrative assistant, treat that person exactly as you would treat the executive.

4. Build your compelling statements around drivers, strategies and critical success factors important to the executive. Show you have done homework.

5. Use a successful reference as a proof statement of your claim. Pick a reference that you think the executive will be impressed with. Have another one or two ready in case the executive is not impressed with your initial one or wants more.

6. Create a sense of urgency by using email or fax to transmit requested information. Use a follow up call to confirm receipt of the information and to try, again, for an appointment.

7. If blocked from meeting the executive, ask to speak to an appropriate subordinate. Make contact with that subordinate, referencing being sent by the executive's office.

8. Be persistent, professional and friendly. You are a capable advisor who has useful information to share with the customer.

DISCUSSION TOPICS

1. For some of your important prospect opportunities, identify who, internally or externally to the account, might introduce you to executives at those accounts. Why should each person you identify be your agent?

2. For each executive identified in Discussion Topic 1, who is the executive's administrative assistant? What can you say to each assistant that will get you past his or her screen?

CHAPTER 6:
PREPARING FOR A DYNAMITE EXECUTIVE MEETING

YOUR RESEARCH IS THE FONT OF IDEAS

" *Joe, let's get ready to make the call to Heather Hanks, the VP of Operations at Churchill. I assume that's who you want to start with.* "

"You bet!"

"OK. To focus our thinking, it'll really help if we recap all the things we've learned about Churchill and Ms. Hanks' operation that might be relevant to making this a dynamite meeting for both you and her.

I'll write on the board. You start talking."

"This I've got to see...ghost writing!

Let me get my marked-up copy of Mr. Profitt's letter and the notes I've made from my web search for Churchill and Heather Hanks.

"Let's start with drivers."

"OK. Last year was difficult for Churchill with a soft economy, but they expect this year's economy to be much better.

Revenues were flat last year, but profits were up. Operating margins were up 15%.

Medicare and Medicaid have reduced their reimbursement rates.

Their two new Centers of Excellence, women's health and digestive disorders, were successes.

How did I do?"

"I think you got all that are relevant to your efforts. Now, what about strategies?"

"OK, let's see what I've marked.

Of course, there are the two cost-cutting and productivity strategies: 'Squeeze it Out' and 'Raise the Bar.' Both were successful last year and are continuing this year. I'm keying my MegaDoppel sales effort to those initiatives.

Churchill is acquiring Miramar to broaden their services and service areas. They intend to keep looking at possible acquisitions like that.

They are planning big time growth of market share in all their services and service areas. They also imply they are going to add new Centers of Excellence. And, they seem to understand that they need new technology in their processes to achieve all that growth.

They have a new cardiology guru who is going to be leading their affiliation with State University. And, they are implementing a six sigma quality program.

They also mentioned a big objective: accelerate the growth of revenue and the census. Obviously, all these strategies are meant to achieve that objective.

What do you think of all that, Sely?"

"Good stuff, Joe. On target. Nice pick-up on the two objectives."

"What do you think is critical to them to achieve their objectives and strategies this year?"

"I would say that quality is critical. They recognize it as a big competitive differentiator.

Of course, continued cost control and productivity gains are critical to being able to move cash into their growth plans."

"I'd add sound leadership, high staff morale, and strong physician endorsement to those critical factors. Churchill is coming out of a rough time. New direction and inspiration of the troops to focus their attentions on implementing the strategies will be fundamental to any success."

"Yeah, I agree. That's probably why they hired Dr. Medicus to the teaching program and Heather Hanks to run operations. Both bring new ideas and new zeal to the hospital.

Speaking of whom, I found Ms. Hank's background interesting in that press release Churchill issued when they hired her. She comes with solid hospital administrative experience. It's particularly interesting that she left a big, prestigious hospital to come to Churchill. Based on her job positions at her previous employer, it looked like she was on a fast track at that hospital. I wonder what caused her to leave?

Plus, she certainly has a good education: master's degree in hospital administration from Duke University. Wow!"

"Maybe if you get to meet her, you might find out more of what motivates her.

What other sales intelligence have you gathered?"

"Well, I also looked at the CFO's resume and that of Mr. Profitt. Then, there's some obvious stuff...$750 million size hospital...3,500 employees...660 beds...the census data. All of those are good sizes for our typical customer. No layoffs, which shows some degree of loyalty to the employees. I've noted their Centers of Excellence. Mr. Profitt, the CEO, almost guaranteed big-time growth and success this year. So, he probably has a lot of heat on the other execs to perform."

"OK, Joe, all that is good information. I'd say you have an excellent base of information to develop a strategy to meet with Ms. Hanks.

What we're going to do next is craft an opening statement which we hope will get Ms. Hanks' attention and intrigue her enough to want to talk more with you. We'll have some additional statements to support and expand your value propositions to her. Then, we'll build a series of questions that you want to ask to get her talking and bring her down the path to what you can do for her and her operations.

Are you ready?"

"You bet. I've been ready for a long time now. You're the one who keeps delaying me."

"Yes, Joe, I know, I know.

Speaking of which, we need to take a little diversion first."

"Now what!?"

REFERENCES: YOUR PROOF STATEMENT

"In your opening statement and in most of your value propositions, you're going to be making claims about what you, your company and your product and services can do for Churchill and Ms. Hanks. How does she know any of that is really true? How does she know your claims aren't just sales hype?"

"Because I don't lie or exaggerate?"

"You may know that, but she doesn't know you.

The best proof is to try out your MegaDoppel for a short time to see if it does what you say it can. But, that really isn't practical. The efforts and expenses by both the hospital and your company to change systems and processes are just too much for a 'test ride.'

So, the next best thing as a proof statement is a good reference, a reference to someone who has already done it and succeeded."

"I knew that."

"Good. Tell me what kind of reference would be the best to use to convince Ms. Hanks that you have something real for her to consider."

"Well, the closer the reference's needs and operations are to her needs and operations, the more convincing it will be. It would be good if the person who she should talk to is someone in the same position as she is. I guess the closer the type of business and the closer the size of the operations would also help."

"You understand the concept of references pretty well.

The more well-known the reference and the more respected it is in the business community, the more persuasive it will be.

It would also be more convincing if you were the one who sold the reference. That would give you a more intimate understanding of the reference's needs and operations.

And, Joe, if I were you, I wouldn't go into the meeting with just one reference, no matter how good I thought it was. Ms. Hanks might reject your main reference for some reason. So, it's best to have one or two backups, just in case."

"Well, I don't personally have any customers that fill the bill. But, there's one in our region sold by one of the other sales reps in our office. It's Century Hospital. They bought a MegaDoppel a year ago for the same reasons that Churchill is looking to upgrade: introduce state-of-the-art technology to improve workflow productivity and quality.

The folks at Century are very proud of their accomplishments with the MegaDoppel. They've been a good reference for other sales reps.

One problem is that Century is about half the size of Churchill. But, if you look at the things the operations people have to do, it's just like Churchill. The management and workflow problems are the same even though the volume of activities might be different.

Yeah, I think Century would be a good one to start with. They aren't exactly a household name, but they are respected in their service area for being an innovator in health care.

I'll check on coming up with a couple of others."

"OK, Century it is. Just be prepared to explain why it's a good reference. The closer the reference is to the criteria, the more compelling the proof.

Now, let's come up with our opening statement for Ms. Hanks."

"Finally!"

A COMPELLING OPENING

"Take a look at the drivers, strategies and critical success factors that we wrote on the board. Which ones really stand out to you as the ones you can impact the most?"

"Clearly the productivity and quality strategies, both of which we also think are critical success factors."

"Well, that answers my second question: Are these really important to the success of Churchill and the targeted executive? If they are CSFs, then by definition, they are really important.

Do you think these strategies are important to Ms. Hanks, personally?"

"Sely, what kind of dumb question is that? Of course, they're important to her. She has the biggest impact on both. She's new to Churchill. Here's the perfect way for her to show Mr. Profitt that he made a great decision hiring her and that he should double her bonus if she can make big improvements in productivity and quality."

"Maybe it's obvious in the case of Ms. Hanks and Churchill, but be careful of assuming. Just because there's a strategy, even a critical one, doesn't mean that all the executives are aligned to it. It's just smart selling to ask the question of yourself before you jump to the so-called obvious conclusion."

"Okay, okay, you made your point. What's next?"

"Just to review, your opening statement should be built around a driver or strategy important to the hospital and to the targeted executive. The more important, the better. The more personally important, the better.

Next, we think about how we can impact that strategy... our value proposition. And, then, we craft the opening statement which includes the strategy, our value proposition, our reference and a question to get the executive talking. Use their own words as much as you can. It's also nice to work in the fact that we've done some homework."

"Knowing your way with words, Sely, I suspect this is no big deal for you. But, to me, it's like speaking in a foreign language. Show me."

"It's really not that difficult.

Start with the driver or strategy that you selected. Maybe something like, 'Ms. Hanks, as I understand it from reading Mr. Profitt's latest letter on Churchill's web site, two big initiatives for this year are increasing productivity and continuing to emphasize quality.'

How does that sound?"

"Nice. You hit the two strategy hot buttons and you implied we did our homework by referencing the letter.

Please continue."

"Also, notice that I used her name and I didn't state the strategies as facts. I discounted my knowledge by saying, 'As I understand it.' That gives Ms. Hanks the opportunity to correct my understanding if I'm wrong. Of course, if I'm wrong at this point in the relationship, there might not be any further relationship. So, you really want to pick pretty solid drivers, strategies and CSFs to base your opening.

Next comes the value proposition followed by the proof statement. Something like, 'We've worked closely with other hospitals like Churchill to significantly enhance their workflow productivity and quality efforts. For example, by implementing our solution, Century Hospital has increased productivity by X% and quality by Y%.'

> **Folks who are persistent, professional, and make a compelling argument of why I must see them, I will eventually grant them a meeting. I never see sales folks just for the sake of seeing them. There must be a relevant business reason and they need to get to the point in about 10 seconds.**
>
> *Chief Procurement Officer*
> *Defense Contractor*

Notice the percentages in the reference. The more specific you can be in the results experienced by the reference, the more believable the reference.

Also notice the word 'enhance.' There are three words you should get used to using: enable, enhance, assist.

'Enable' means 'You really can't do it without me.' 'Enhance' means 'You could do it without me, but I can add so much value to the effort, why would you want to do it without me?' 'Assist' means 'I'm a strategic part of the solution.'

Notice that the interpretations get weaker as you go down the list.

So, Joe, if you can really be an enabler for a hospital, that's a very strong value proposition. Being an enhancement is strong, but not as strong as enabler. And, the weakest position is being an assist, but if that's all you have, then you have to play that card.

In the case of Churchill, I don't think you can claim that you are an enabler. They've already demonstrated that they can improve productivity and quality without you. But, with your MegaDoppel, maybe you can be a big enhancement to those efforts."

"You bet we can. I agree that they can do some improvements without us, but we can really accelerate that effort and give them more of it. So, enhancement is right."

"Which brings up a couple of additional words that are examples of enhancement: accelerate, multiply. Other

nice values you can use are making the prospect more agile and getting their services faster to the market.

The point is to use language that stirs a strong reaction on the part of the listener. But, be careful what you claim. You must be able to back up the claim."

"This is good stuff, Sely. I think I can do this."

"The last piece of the opening is a question to get Ms. Hanks talking. A very useful question is one that asks her to comment on what she thinks of your value proposition. It might be something like, 'Would those enhancements be important to you and your operations here at Churchill?'

Hopefully for you, she'll be thrilled with the opportunity. Depending on what she says, you have to be prepared with the next level of questions, which is our next topic.

But let me summarize the technique for developing a compelling opening statement.

First, pick a compelling driver, strategy or critical success factor that is particularly important to the target executive and one that you can significantly impact. Start your statement with your understanding of that need.

Next, provide your value proposition on how you can impact that need. Follow that immediately with the reference proof statement.

End with a question to get the executive talking and reacting to your value proposition.

Of course, all of this has to be customized to your own style and how you talk."

"I like it, Sely. I really like it. It gives me the way to open a conversation with an executive, something I've always feared. It's coming together...how I'm a business advisor, an expert in my business that can help an executive in his or her business."

Most successful salespeople make it impossible for me not to agree to a meeting, because the reasons are so compelling enough that I am almost afraid *not* to meet.

CIO
Retailer

"Joe, it's possible that Ms. Hanks may not be interested in your opening value proposition. In the case of Churchill, that's unlikely unless they've already committed to Super Solutions. But, with another prospect, the problem might be that you may not have as good information on the hospital as we have with Churchill, so your opening may not be as accurate.*

If the executive rejects your opening as not important enough to get his or her attention, then you have to have a backup value proposition or you'll be quickly dismissed. Now, this can be a little touchy. You don't want to be perceived as going on a fishing expedition with the executive.

One approach is to ask what issues or challenges the executive is particularly concerned with in achieving the enterprise's strategies. But, that's a blank-page question...highly risky.

Possibly better is to have a second driver, strategy or critical success factor in mind with a value proposition for that. What might that be for Ms. Hanks?"

"Umm. Looking at what we have on the board, maybe the inventory problem they have in coordinating operations across long-distance locations is something we can help them with."

"Good. Give me an opening statement for that need."

"Let me see. How's this: 'Ms. Hanks, in Mr. Profitt's letter, it seems that a major strategy is increasing the presence of Churchill across the state. We've been able to help hospitals with far-flung operations like Churchill better control the workflow process and coordination so that the hospital is more agile in handling varying volume demands. At XYZ hospital, we reduced their costs by A% by tailoring the workflow standards to their varying census volumes at each of their six locations. Would that be something important for you?'

How's that?"

"Pretty good. You might try to shorten it a little. If it's too long, you risk losing the attention of your listener. And, of course, you would need a real reference.

My guess is that, with that opening, the executive would probably ask for more details on exactly what you're talking about. That's a perfect and very desirable result...getting the executive to ask you for more information. The more he or she asks, the more opportunity you have to sell."

Speaking of questions, we're now ready to develop our own. There are basically two sets of questions that you want to ask: things you want to know and things you want the executive to think about.

The first set is pretty easy to define. What do you want to know from Ms. Hanks, Joe?"

"First, I want to know if I still have a shot at the business.

If the answer to that is, 'No,' then I don't have any more questions to ask."

"Unless they've placed an order with Super Solutions, then the answer to that question is more in your hands than hers.

What else do you want to know, assuming you're still in the ball game?"

"I need to know if they're willing to spend more than what they now have in their budget. I need to understand what are the really important criteria that they'll use to make their decision. That'll tell me how committed they are or aren't to Super Solutions.

I also want to know what I have to do to get a fair shot with my proposal. And, when are they going to make the decision.

How's that for my questions?"

"It seems to me that most of the answers that you'll get depend on how well you sell your solution.

Just make sure that, when you go into the meeting, you have your questions written on a piece of paper so that you can make sure you don't forget one. That's part of being prepared...having notes.

Let's turn to the other set of questions, the ones we want to ask that'll get the executive talking and thinking. Again, you'll want to have these written down in your notes so that you have them ready to use when the opportunities arise.

One type of question is simply to get the executive's reaction. We already used one in the opening statement about what Ms. Hanks thinks about your productivity and quality value propositions.

What other ones can you think of that you might want to ask somewhere in the conversation?"

"I want to know what she thinks of Super Solutions and their stuff."

"How would you ask her that?"

"I just did. Didn't you hear me?"

"Umm. Another way you might phrase it so as not to look like you're afraid of your competition is, 'Ms. Hanks, I know you are considering other possible solutions to your needs. What have you seen that you like? What

haven't you seen that you want?' You might want to write that one down.

What else?"

"Nothing I can think of right now. Tell me about the other questions you're talking about."

The quickest way to lose the sale and my respect is to waste my time on stupid questions about my business. I hate that.

CIO
Retailer

"OK. These are questions that either raise anxiety and questions that paint the picture of what might be possible. Either way, they can be powerful in getting the executive involved and intrigued with what you have to offer.

An anxiety-producing question might be, 'Ms. Hanks, what would it mean to Churchill's business if the quality of the services doesn't significantly improve?'

A question that paints the possibilities might be, 'Ms. Hanks, how would increasing workflow throughput by 10% without increasing operating costs impact Churchill?'

The key is to base the questions on real needs or values that your solution can readily address, especially where you have a strong competitive advantage. You're cultivating those advantages into decision criteria and cost justifications. You're getting the executive to commit to the degree of importance of the particular aspect you're raising. This is dynamite input for your proposal.

Now, it's your turn. What anxiety or possibility questions do you want to raise with Ms. Hanks?"

"How about, 'Ms. Hanks, what would happen if the solution you pick doesn't meet your expectations?' That should put fear in her heart if she plans to buy Super Solutions."

"Joe, you're obsessed with your competitor. I hope this obsession doesn't show in your meeting with Ms. Hanks, assuming you get one.

How about a more customer-focused question?"

" 'Ms. Hanks, what would it mean to Churchill to achieve six sigma quality in your processes and services?' "

"Good one. More?"

" 'Ms. Hanks, how important is it to your future plans to be able to standardize your workflow processes?'

With the MegaDoppel, they can standardize the processes across the whole network of locations and still customize for the volume differences. It's a big selling point.

Here's another: 'Ms. Hanks, how will you cope with the increased demand for services expected by Mr. Profitt?'

I want her to visualize people going crazy in the halls as they try to cope with all the patient demands. We can do a lot for her in better managing workflow to meet a changing volume.

Do these questions do what you want?"

"A better question, Joe, is, do these questions do what you want? They're certainly good examples of what I'm talking about. Raise anxieties and paint the possibilities to plant decision criteria and cost justifications and to set the base for strong competitive differentiation for you and your products and services.

Write down the questions you've formulated. Give it some more thought. Make sure you go into the meeting with a healthy set of information gathering and anxiety and possibility questions."

"OK, Sely, I see the importance of doing this. I don't want to forget something important. I'll only have one or two shots at seeing her."

HOW LONG TO MEET

"Which brings up another point. How long do you think you will have to meet with Ms. Hanks, again, assuming you get the appointment?"

"I don't know. She'll probably let me know how much time she has."

"That's certainly possible; however, if you're a confident business advisor, you should be advising her as to how much time you think a meeting should take to cover the important issues.

In my experience, it's typical to ask for and to expect 20-30 minutes. That means you have to really be sharp in what you want to accomplish and how you do it. Hence the need for all this careful preparation.

But, it's possible the meeting could go longer if she gets interested. So, the axiom is to expect 20 minutes and be prepared for an hour.

Prioritize your points and questions. During the meeting, be flexible to go with the interests of the executive as long as it's producing value for both of you. You can always redirect the conversation by asking one of your questions.

It's also smart, once you have the appointment, to confirm it with the executive, maybe by email or a short note. In that note, it's wise to give the executive a little taste of the purpose of the meeting. Don't fire all your ammunition. Just a little nugget to whet the person's interest and get him or her thinking.

For example, in your note to Ms. Hanks, you might say, 'I look forward to meeting you and reviewing with you some critical, new information that could make a significant difference in your workflow upgrade project.' Now, that 'critical, new information' could be anything. It could be the Century reference, maybe even the possibility of a visit to Century."

"I like that idea about a visit to Century. Yeah, that's really good."

KNOW THE PERSON

"It will really help you to craft your call strategy if you know something about the executive's personality.

What do you know about Ms. Hanks?"

"Not a whole lot. I already told you about what I read in the press release when she joined Churchill. From that, I'd say she was certainly an achiever. Sam, the one guy on the committee who has been friendly to me, says that she's a no-nonsense person. Other than that, I don't know anything else about her.

Why does it make a difference?"

"It could make a big difference. You don't have a lot of time in a first-time visit to show the executive what a nice person you are. What you don't want to happen is for the executive to take an instant dislike to you. So, knowing something about the executive's personality and style allows you to tailor your approach a little to smooth the interaction toward the style of the executive.

Now, you have your own personality and style. You definitely don't want to go into the meeting with a phony personality or style. The executive will see through that right away. What I'm talking about is just a little adjusting to the style of the executive."

"How do I decide what to adjust?"

"In general, there are two styles to think about: analytical and emotional. Now, this isn't to say that every

executive falls into one or the other of those buckets. But, for our purposes of planning and conducting sales calls, we can characterize them into one of those two descriptions.

The analytical type is a no-nonsense, very task-oriented, get-down-to-the-facts, make-a-decision-and-move-on-type person. The emotional type tends to be more easygoing, not so much in a hurry, let's-get-to-know-each-other-type person. This in no way implies that an analytical executive is better than an emotional one. It's just a question of style."

"Of the two, I'd say Ms. Hanks is definitely analytical. So, what's that mean to how I conduct my sales call with her?"

"Well, for starters, I wouldn't spend a lot of time trying to build nice, comfy rapport with her. I'd open the call with a little pleasantry to set a positive tone, and then, I'd get right down to business unless, of course, she prolonged the pleasantries.

During the balance of the call, I'd maintain a business demeanor and not stray from the main issues unless she raised sidetracks. Keep your presentation uncluttered. Make it easy for her to understand what you are saying and offering so that she can quickly evaluate and make a decision.

I'd also keep very close track of time, so that I didn't violate the agreed upon length of the call unless she extended it.

With an analytical executive, keep it crisp and to the point."

"How's it different with an emotional one? They're all busy."

"With an emotional type, I'd be prepared to extend the rapport building so that the executive could learn more about me and my personality. I wouldn't be as intense in my demeanor and presentation as I would with an analytical person. I might venture into sidetracks to see how the executive reacts.

Emotional style executives are more likely to respond to things that are exciting and less likely to respond to highly detailed, analytical dissertations. So, put some passion into your presentation when meeting an emotional type.

It's just a small nuance, but it could have a huge impact."

"OK, I can see how it could make a difference. It's one more thing I've got to add to my checklist of things to be prepared for the call."

BE PREPARED IN MANY WAYS

"And, Joe, be prepared, not only with your opening and your questions and some knowledge about the executive. Also bring all the account documentation with you. If she asks you a question, you want to have the necessary reference material to answer her. You want to look like you have things under control."

"Maybe I should bring my manager with me."

"Who you bring to the meeting is a function of what you're trying to accomplish. If you need your manager there to show your company's commitment or to negotiate a specific contractual point, then bring your manager. Just make sure you control the meeting, otherwise you're seen as an errand boy. Kings only talk to pages when they want the page to fetch something. You want to be seen as a knight, not a page.

In general, the fewer the people from your company the better, even if the executive loads up the meeting with other people from his or her company."

"It's just nice to have the moral support of someone else there."

"Get your confidence from your preparation and belief in what you can do for the prospect, not from someone who will have little to add or, worse yet, take over the call from you.

Speaking of being confidently prepared, it's a good idea to do a little rehearsing, especially with your opening statement so that it comes out smoothly and confidently. There's where you can use your manager or a fellow sales rep, or even your own executives if the account is important enough. They could even do a little role-playing, responding to your statement in different ways to give you some practice in handling those reactions.

Finally, and this is so important, possibly more than anything else we've talked about: Be yourself. Don't try to be something you just aren't. An executive will quickly see past that façade.

All the techniques we've talked about are just that, techniques. They aren't you and what you bring to the table. Yes, these techniques help you to better express your ideas and direct the executive's considerations to things you believe are important. But, people buy from people. Be yourself.

And, Joe?"

"Yeah?"

"Smile. Not like a Cheshire cat but, rather, with a genuine, friendly smile."

"Look, I'm smiling. Can I make the call to Ms. Hanks now?"

"Let's just summarize what we've talked about so that you have a complete list to refer to as you prepare for your call."

REVIEW KEY POINTS

1. Start your preparation by collecting all your sales intelligence into one place:

    - Prospect's drivers, strategies, critical success factors
    - Background on the executives
    - Size, trend and comparison data

2. Select the driver, strategy and/or critical success factor which you can impact the most. Make sure your choice is important to the hospital and to the targeted executive. Define your value proposition as to how you impact the selected driver, strategy and/or CSF.

3. Assemble a compelling set of references as proof statements of what you can do. The closer to the following criteria, the better:

    - Excellent, measurable results from using your solution
    - Same needs and processes as your prospect
    - Same type of business as your prospect
    - Same size and volumes as your prospect
    - Contact person at the reference has the same job and responsibilities as your targeted executive
    - Reference is a prestigious, highly-respected enterprise
    - You sold the solution to the reference

4. Craft your opening statement:

   State your understanding of the driver/strategy/CSF.

   State your value proposition. Use words and phrases like:

   • Enhance
   • Assist
   • Accelerate
   • Multiply
   • More agile
   • Faster time-to-market

   Provide a quick description of your reference and the results the reference achieved using your solution.

   End with a question to solicit the executive's reaction.

   Be ready with a backup statement if the executive discounts your opening.

5. Develop a set of questions to ask. Write the questions in your meeting notes.

   • Questions that provide you with sales intelligence
   • "What do you think?" questions to solicit the executive's reaction and interest
   • "What if?" questions to create anxiety for failure
   • "What if?"questions to paint the possibilities of success

   Focus your "what if?" questions on key values of your solution, especially strong competitive differentiators.

DISCUSSION POINTS

1. Using a prospect for whom you have done research and for whom you have targeted executives you want to visit, select one of those executives, and using the Key Point guidance above, prepare a compelling opening statement and backup statement.

   Try your statements with another sales rep or your manager. Get their advice as to how to strengthen the statements. Role play different reactions to the statements so that you can prepare for those eventualities.

2. For the same executive you selected in Discussion Point 1, prepare a set of questions. Have another sales rep or your manager react to your 'what if' questions to strengthen them.

3. How would you characterize the personality and style of this executive?

CHAPTER 7:
HOW TO CONDUCT
THE EXECUTIVE CALL

HAVE AN ATTITUDE

"*O*K, now what do you have to say that's keeping me from getting my appointment at Churchill?"

"First, Joe, I want to make sure you go into this effort with the right attitude."

The trust thing is huge to me with sales folks whom I deal with. I trust the ones that do what they say they will do and who don't over promise what they can do. A salesperson that I like to deal with is sincere with me and clearly articulates his company's capabilities without all the embellishments that many sales folks like to do.

Vice President, Operations
Financial Investment
Company

"My attitude is great. I'm going to show them how dumb it is to buy Super Solutions."

"Umm. Let's step back for a moment.

Remember, you've done homework. From your review of the annual report and what you already know from your involvement with Churchill, you have a pretty good initial understanding of their business and the drivers, strategies and critical success factors that concern the executives. You've prepared your opening statement and have written your questions, including the 'what ifs.'*

I've been assuming all along that you know your MegaDoppel and how it can be used effectively by Churchill. Am I right in assuming that?"

"You can bet on that, Sely. I know our products and services very well. And I know exactly how Churchill can use the MegaDoppel to great advantage. I've done my homework and I'm ready."

"Good. That's the kind of attitude you'll need: confident, but not so confident that you're cocky. You're the expert in your business. Churchill needs you and that expertise. Just don't shove it down their throats with salt.

I would say that trust and credibility of the salesperson are very key to me for doing business with a company. I always buy from people that I like, and never from those that I don't like.

CEO
Financial Institution

Keep in mind that people buy from people. And, they buy more often from people that they like and trust. So, Joe, be a likable person and be trustworthy. Don't exaggerate. Be honest in your assessment of Churchill's needs and how good your MegaDoppel fits those needs. And, be positive, not a sore loser looking to show them how dumb they are."

"OK, OK. Am I ready now?"

"If you believe you're ready, then pick up the telephone and go for it!"

"Finally!

OK, here I go." (Dialing)

[Operator:] "Good Morning, Churchill. How may I direct your call?"

"Good morning. Ms. Hanks, please."

[Kathy, Ms. Hanks' administrative assistant:] "Good morning. Ms. Hanks' office. Kathy speaking."

"Good morning, Kathy, this is Joe Repp of Mega Systems. I'm calling for Ms. Hanks."

[Kathy:] "Is she expecting your call?"

"I'm currently working with some of her team investigating a new workflow system. I thought it would be important for Ms. Hanks to have some first-hand input from me regarding how the selection process is going."

[Kathy:] "Uh. Well, Ms. Hanks is currently in a meeting and her schedule is very tight all day. If you give me your telephone number, I'll let her know that you called."

"Hold the phone right there! Joe, do you think you gave Kathy a very compelling reason for you to have access to Ms. Hanks?"

"Yeah. It's exactly what Ms. Hanks needs to hear."

"That may be true, but do you think that Ms. Hanks wants to hear from you how her people are doing the job she assigned them? That strikes me as a very risky

proposition. She probably thinks she's plenty capable of assessing her own people without your help."

"Well, you said I should be an advisor. I'm advising."

"I thought you did your homework and had a good opening statement. Can you maybe think of a less risky and possibly more compelling reason to give Kathy to get her to place a higher priority on your request for an audience?"

"Well, maybe I can build on the need for efficiency and quality and the results of our installation at Century. I have an open invitation to bring prospects over there. They like to show off their operation."

"Now, that's certainly less risky and it sounds more compelling. Let's reset the clock and try again."

[Kathy:] "Good morning. Ms. Hanks' office. Kathy speaking."

"Good morning, Kathy, this is Joe Repp of Mega Systems. I'm calling for Ms. Hanks."

[Kathy:] "Is she expecting your call?"

"I'm currently working with some of her team investigating a new workflow system. I have a timely opportunity for Ms. Hanks to visit Century Hospital to see how they tackled their needs to increase productivity and improve process quality. Based on my understanding of the situation in Churchill's operations, these are similar challenges that Ms. Hanks faces. Is she in today?"

[Kathy:] "Well, Ms. Hanks is currently in a meeting and her schedule is very tight all day. Exactly where is Century located? And when did you have such a visit in mind?"

I trust salespeople that don't try to blow smoke, and that is tentative until they do what they say they are going to do. Sometimes, it is just the little things like a promised article or coffee cup or a follow-up email.

Vice President, Marketing
Airline

"OK, Joe, now you have Kathy thinking. Help her to help you. Make it easy for Ms. Hanks to visit Century."

"Kathy, I know Ms. Hanks is very busy with many high priority needs. But, as I understand it, the challenges in the Churchill operations are also very high on her list of priorities. I have some very useful information that could make a major difference for her and Churchill.

I can set up this visit to Century at Ms. Hanks' convenience, but it should be done this week or next. It can even be after Churchill's normal business hours. I will pick her up and bring her back. The drive to Century is about 20 minutes."

[Kathy:] "Well, please give me your telephone number, Mr. Repp. I'll review what you have described with Ms. Hanks and get back to you later today."

"To help you, Kathy, I'll email you a description of what we just discussed. What's your email address?"

[Kathy:] "Yes, that would be helpful. My email is..."

"OK, Joe, that was quite professional and helpful."

"But I don't have the appointment."

"C'mon, be real! Did you expect everyone at Churchill to immediately halt what they were doing so that they could meet with you? You gave Kathy good ammunition and you've sent an email with the details to avoid any confusion. You have a commitment from Kathy to get back to you later today. If she doesn't call, you can follow up tomorrow morning with her. She now owes you a response."

> **Trust is something that I try to give everybody that is not an outwardly fool from the beginning. But, only a few salespeople have the character to keep it. Those that do, I conduct business with.**
>
> *CIO*
> *Retailer*

"Well, let's see if she does call. This waiting is killing me."

WHAT TO EXPECT

"To give you something useful to do while you wait, let's talk about what might happen when you finally talk with Ms. Hanks."

"Must we?"

"Yes, Joe, we must.

First, establish some rapport with her, but, given what we know of her analytical style, keep the small talk to a minimum unless she prolongs it.

Keep in mind that she's a very busy person. Her attention span may be very short. She may also have a very short-term memory. This all means that you have to be clear in your presentation, relating it constantly to her situation. It also means you should occasionally summarize your salient points and get her concurrence that she understands and agrees.

As we talked about before, be careful making declarative statements about her business. Frame your understanding as just that: your understanding based on what you have read or what you have heard from credible sources. Ask her to confirm your understanding. She'll either confirm it or correct it.

In the beginning, you'll probably have to carry the conversation. She'll be evaluating you to decide whether you have something to offer her or if it's a waste of time.

Get her talking about her operation. Ask your prepared questions that show you have an understanding of her business and how you and Mega Systems can help her."

(Telephone rings.)

"Excuse me. That might be Kathy.

Good afternoon, Joe Repp speaking."

[Kathy:] "Mr. Repp, this is Kathy, Ms. Hanks' assistant."

"Hello, Kathy. Thank you for calling."

[Kathy:] "Yes. I showed Ms. Hanks your email. She has a question to ask you. Can you speak with her now?"

"Uh...sure...sure I can."

"Be confident, Joe. You're an expert. Ms. Hanks needs information. Think before you talk. Use your opening statement."

[Ms. Hanks:] "Mr. Repp, this is Heather Hanks. I understand that you have been working with some of my people on our workflow upgrade project. I also understand from Kathy that you would like me to visit Century Hospital. What would I gain from such a visit?"

"Well, Ms. Hanks, as I understand the challenges at Churchill, increasing workflow efficiency while improving process quality are critical success factors for the hospital. Is that correct?"

[Ms. Hanks:] "Yes. Both are very important, but not at any price. We must achieve those results while still maintaining our budgets. Now, what would I see at Century that would help me to do just that?"

"Ms. Hanks, I fully appreciate the need to maintain budgets, but don't you think that a more important issue is return on investment?"

"Stop the action!

Joe, what are you doing? You had her moving in your direction and now you want to start an argument on budgets and return on investment?"

"Yeah, well, that's the real issue, isn't it."

"It may well be, but you have barely spoken with Ms. Hanks. You haven't met her. You haven't established your credentials. Now is a very risky time to be talking money."

"She brought it up. I didn't."

> In my business trust is everything. As a bank, everything we do conveys trust to our customers. Losing that trust means losing business. The same is true with a salesperson.
>
> **CEO**
> **Bank**

"Yes, she did bring it up. You can address it later when you have established your own bona fides and the values of your offering. The real issue right now is to get an appointment to do just those things, either with or without a visit to Century.

Now, let's re-do that last bit."

[Ms. Hanks:] "Yes. Both are very important, but not at any price. We must achieve those results while still maintaining our budgets. Now, what would I see at Century that would help me to do just that?"

"Ms. Hanks, I certainly appreciate the need to be fiscally sound. That's part of what you will see at Century: how they tackled a very challenging situation in their workflow to increase productivity and improve quality without overextending their available budget. Before making those changes, Century was losing significant market share. Now, they have recaptured that lost share and are even taking share away from their competitors because Century is more cost-competitive and has excellent quality."

[Ms. Hanks:] "Mr. Repp, I'm sure that Century has done just what you say. But, maybe it would be better if we spent a few minutes together so that I can better understand what you are proposing before we invest the time and effort to go to Century. Would you be available tomorrow afternoon, say at 2 PM?"

"Yes, I am, Ms. Hanks. I'll see you then."

"Congratulations, Joe. You have achieved the first big step in your quest. You have an appointment with Ms. Hanks, VP of Operations, at Churchill. You gave her a good reason to meet with you...at least, you did after we had a couple of discussions and re-dos. You were professional. You were positive. You were a confident advisor.

Now, you have to prepare for tomorrow's meeting so that you also show that you are trustworthy."

"I can do this. I can do it. Just watch!"

"I will, Joe. I will."

"EXECU-SPEAK" 101

(Next day; lobby at Churchill Hospital.)

"Hello, Joe. All set for your visit with Ms. Hanks?"

"What are you doing here? Go away. I'm busy psyching myself up."

"Good idea. Not me going away...you psyching yourself up...to be a confident, trustworthy and knowledgeable advisor."

"I know, I know. Just be quiet, please. And wait here. I don't want you doing your strange stuff while I'm talking with Ms. Hanks."

"Strange stuff? You mean like stopping and resetting the clock? Only if it's absolutely necessary.

Now, Joe, don't forget. As soon as you walk into her office, you'll have clues about her. Look around. Be alert to the little things. Open with a little, very little, rapport building unless she prolongs it."

"Go away."

"Don't worry, she can't see me."

[Receptionist] "Mr. Repp, Ms. Hanks will see you now."

"OK. Thanks."

(Walks into Ms. Hanks' office.)

"Good afternoon, Ms. Hanks. I'm Joe Repp."

[Ms. Hanks:] "Good afternoon, Joe. May I call you Joe?"

"Certainly."

[Ms. Hanks:] "And, please, call me Heather. Sit down. Would you like some coffee?"

"Only if you are having some."

(Ms. Hanks asks Kathy to bring them coffee.)

"Joe, look at this office. It's very simple. Nothing fancy for her. Just a couple of family pictures on the credenza. Otherwise, this is the office of someone who rolls up her sleeves and digs in. You might want to keep the small talk short. Get right down to business."

"Ms. Hanks, I certainly appreciate you taking time to meet with me. I realize you are very busy. I'll try to make good use our of time together.

I represent Mega Systems. We are one of the suppliers that your committee is considering to automate your workflow processes. Mega is a worldwide provider of such systems. It's our principal business.

Based on my earlier meetings with your staff and what I've read in Mr. Profitt's latest letter on Churchill's web site (pulling out the marked up letter from his briefcase), it appears that this workflow project is very critical to Churchill's future competitiveness in the marketplace."

[Heather:] "Yes, Joe, it is certainly that. By the way, I've asked Bob Gross to join us. He should be here momentarily.'

"Oh, oh. Time out.

Is Bob Gross on the committee? Is he the one of those who has been giving you the cold shoulder?"

"Yeah. He's not only on the committee. He runs it. And, yeah, he's been nothing but one big pain. I'm sure he and that Super Solutions guy are in cahoots. What am I going to do now, Mr. Smart Guy?"

"Well, when we were talking about the end-around strategy, I warned you that the executive might bring one of her subordinates into the meeting.

Now, to begin, you're going to continue being a confident, trustworthy and knowledgeable advisor. Number two, you'll be friendly and cordial to Mr. Gross. Remember, he's Heather's subordinate. She knows him. She doesn't know you.

Be careful how you answer any objections that Mr. Gross raises. You can't be seen as an antagonist. You're an advisor who brings valuable opportunities for Heather to consider.

Keep it positive. Get Heather talking. Use your prepared questions, especially the 'what ifs.' Then sell with your ears."

"Sell with my ears? What's that mean?"

"Listen, and listen carefully. The more the customer talks, the more you'll learn that you can build upon."

[Heather:] "Ah, here's Bob now. Bob, I think you know Joe Repp?"

[Bob:] "Yeah. We've had some meetings with him."

"Good afternoon, Bob. I was just remarking to Heather that I appreciate that this workflow project is very critical to Churchill's competitive success. That's why I thought it might help if I introduced her to the people at Century Hospital who have experienced a similar need."

[Bob:] "Who's Century?"

"Bob, Century is a major regional care provider in the next state. They've been a MegaDoppel user for the last year. Their results with the MegaDoppel have been outstanding. And, since they faced similar needs as you here at Churchill, I thought a meeting between Heather and the Century operations management would add useful input to your effort."

[Bob:] "I'll bet you do. Unless they are as big as we are and have the same Centers of Excellence, I don't see what good such a visit would do."

> Trust is something that is critical to a long term relationship, especially if it is indeed strategic to the enterprise. If I let them get their foot in the door for a chance to become a strategic partner, then they had better do what they say they're going to do, or the door will shut on them very quickly, and they will never become strategic to me.
>
> **Chief Procurement Officer**
> **Defense Contractor**

"Careful, Joe. Don't rise to the bait. Continue to consult."

"Bob, they are about half the size of Churchill. But, both of you are geographically dispersed and you both have major Centers of Excellence. They are also growing very rapidly. Like you, they needed to accelerate workflow throughput. There are many similarities when it comes to managing the operations. And, the similarities continue, especially, when you add quality control. Why..."

[Heather (interrupting):] Bob, I think that Joe has a good point. Managing a hospital operation in one place has a lot of commonality with another, especially if there is similarity in the geographic distribution and the types of services offered. It remains to be seen if the volume differences reduce the value of Century's experience to us. Now, Joe, you said that the people at Century achieved outstanding results. What do you mean by outstanding?

"They improved their overall workflow by almost 10% and their process quality is now in the six sigma range.

They are thrilled with those returns on investment. Would those levels of improvement be desirable at Churchill?"

[Heather:] "Are you guaranteeing these results for us?"

"Well, I can't guarantee that your operations will achieve those levels, but based on what I've learned about your operations in the last couple of months working with Bob and his team, significant improvements are achievable. I suspect you also believe so, otherwise, you wouldn't be spending all the energy of your people investigating alternative systems.

Now, one thing I'm very certain about and am willing to guarantee, is that implementing a MegaDoppel solution will provide more throughput and better quality than the other supplier you are considering. We have demonstrated that time and again with many workflow benchmarks."

[Bob:] "Yeah, but at what price. A MegaDoppel will kill our budget.'

"Heather, Bob is right about the MegaDoppel being higher than what you have currently allocated in your budget. But I wonder what you consider to be a good trade-off between the investment and the possible returns on that investment."

[Heather:] Well, we established that budget based on some initial estimates of potential improvements. If you can demonstrate significantly better improvements with a quick payback, then I suspect we could consider such an alternative. But, Joe, I expect proven results, not guesses. And, the payback has to be quick...less than 12 months."

"I think we can make a compelling case for just that."

[Heather:] "OK, Joe. Why don't you give me the name and telephone number of the operations manager at Century. I'll give him a call and have a chat with him. In the meantime, put together your proposal and give it to Bob. Let's see some substance."

"It would be my pleasure. I have Frank Davis' telephone number right here for you. He's Century's Chief Operating Officer. I'll have a proposal to Bob by next Tuesday. And I'll follow up with you to see how your conversation goes with Frank."

[Heather:] "I have a meeting to go to. Thank you for stopping by, Joe."

"Well, congratulations, Joe. You did an excellent job: confident, not cocky, positive and a real businessman. I think Heather was impressed, otherwise she wouldn't have asked for your proposal.

Notice that you didn't have to get into a lot of details with Heather. She's interested in the big picture. Like most executives, she leaves the details to her subordinates.

At a meeting like the one you just had, executives look for several things. They first want to measure you: are you the type of person they want to deal with? Profes-

sional? Knowledgeable? Do you listen? Are you trust-worthy with confidential information?

Do you have an understanding of their business and how you can impact it? Do you really add value with a good grasp of the situation and good ideas to address it?

They want to know if you are honest. Do you exagger-ate or color the truth? Do you tell the bad as well as the good?

They also want to know if you are in a position to make things happen or are you just an errand boy.

Another thing is how well do you work with the executive's staff."

"Well, how do you think I measured up?"

"All in all, pretty good.

You were certainly professional in not rising to Bob's barbs. And, you listened and responded with good busi-ness knowledge to both Heather's and Bob's comments.

Introducing the idea of significantly increasing the re-turns on investment with a MegaDoppel versus the Super Solutions product certainly showed business acumen. Your reference to Century's experience was an excellent proof statement. You made it relevant by focusing on the management of the process instead of the volume of the process. Heather liked that.

You asked two dynamite 'what if' questions, the one about Churchill getting the same results as Century and the one about justifying a budget increase. You didn't use any anxiety questions, but given the positive direction of the call, they didn't seem to be needed.

You were honest in admitting that the MegaDoppel would cost more and was even beyond her current budget, but you were willing to cost-justify that increase. Of course, Heather is now expecting a substantial increase in returns at not so substantial an increase in budget. And, she has made clear that she wants a fast payback.

Whether or not you can work with Bob and the others on the committee is yet to be seen, but Heather is giving you the chance to show that you can. And time will tell whether you can make things happen, but the impression is that you are not just an errand boy.

So, on the whole, an excellent start.

I also like the way you kept the door open to contact Heather by following up on her planned conversation with Frank at Century. Nice move."

"See, Sely, I'm not as dumb as you think."

"Joe, I've never thought you were dumb. You just needed a little coaching and an opportunity to prove to yourself that these techniques really do work.

Now, of course, you will be sending Heather a thank-you note, right?"

"Uh. Right. Right. Of course, I will.

But, now, will you please disappear so I can get to work on that proposal?"

"Yes, Joe, I will do just that."

REVIEW KEY POINTS

1. Build confidence and trust by using your homework. Relate your presentation to the executive's drivers, strategies and critical success factors.

2. Tell the truth. Don't exaggerate. Be honest by telling the bad with the good.

3. Be a positive, can-do and take-charge person. Don't be cocky or flippant.

4. How executives will measure you:

   Do you understand the executive's business sufficiently to be able to make intelligent recommendations? Have you done your homework before meeting the executive?

   Do you know what you are talking about? How long have you been in the business?

   Do you have something new to offer?

   Are you professional and confident?

   Are you an effective communicator?

   Can you really make things happen or are you just an errand runner?

   Are you responsive and timely?

   Do you (can you) work well with the executive's staff and others in the hospital?

   Are your references impressive and relevant?

   Are you respectful of the executive's time and that of the staff?

   Are you action-oriented?

DON'T BE INTIMIDATED!